JOHN KEY

PORTRAIT OF A PRIME MINISTER

JOHN KEY

PORTRAIT OF A PRIME MINISTER

JOHN ROUGHAN

PENGUIN BOOKS

PENGUIN BOOKS
Published by the Penguin Group
Penguin Group (NZ), 67 Apollo Drive, Rosedale,
Auckland 0632, New Zealand (a division of Penguin New Zealand Pty Ltd)
Penguin Group (USA) Inc, 375 Hudson Street,
New York, New York 10014, USA
Penguin Group (Canada), 90 Eglinton Avenue East, Suite 700, Toronto,
Ontario, M4P 2Y3, Canada (a division of Penguin Canada Books Inc.)
Penguin Books Ltd, 80 Strand, London, WC2R 0RL, England
Penguin Ireland, 25 St Stephen's Green,
Dublin 2, Ireland (a division of Penguin Books Ltd)
Penguin Group (Australia), 707 Collins Street, Melbourne,
Victoria 3008, Australia (a division of Penguin Australia Pty Ltd)
Penguin Books India Pvt Ltd, 11, Community Centre,
Panchsheel Park, New Delhi – 110 017, India
Penguin Books (South Africa) (Pty) Ltd, Block D, Rosebank Office Park,
181 Jan Smuts Avenue, Parktown North, Gauteng 2193, South Africa
Penguin (Beijing) Ltd, 7F, Tower B, Jiaming Center, 27 East Third Ring Road North,
Chaoyang District, Beijing 100020, China

Penguin Books Ltd, Registered Offices: 80 Strand, London, WC2R 0RL, England

First published by Penguin Group (NZ), 2014
1 3 5 7 9 10 8 6 4 2

Copyright © John Roughan, 2014

The right of John Roughan to be identified as the author of this work in terms of
section 96 of the Copyright Act 1994 is hereby asserted.

Designed and typeset by Sarah Healey, © Penguin Group (NZ)
Cover image by Mark Mitchell
Cover design by Cameron Gibb
Printed and bound in Australia by Griffin Press,
an Accredited ISO AS/NZS 14001 Environmental Management Systems Printer

ISBN 978-0-143-57075-2

A catalogue record for this book is available
from the National Library of New Zealand.

www.penguin.co.nz

MIX
Paper from
responsible sources
FSC® C009448

Contents

Author's Note   7
Introduction   9

1. Broken Home   17
2. Poor Boy?   27
3. Ruth   37
4. Growing Up   49
5. Currency Dealer   63
6. London, New York   75
7. Down and Dirty   91
8. Rapid Rise   105
9. 'Crony Capitalist'   117
10. Rebranding National   129
11. Road to Victory   141
12. Inside the Beehive   151
13. Partners in Power   163
14. Popular Joker   177
15. Seismic and Fiscal Shocks   189
16. Commanding Trust   201
17. Not a Job for Life   215
18. A Time to Assess   229

Acknowledgements   245
Index   247
About the Author   255

Author's Note

Politics is the cruellest of careers. Those elected to its highest office must endure constant criticism for as long as they retain the country's confidence and can expect to be regarded at best with public indifference once their time has passed. This book aims to illuminate the life and politics of a Prime Minister at the height of his power. It might have been possible to tell the story without his co-operation but it would have lacked his voice and struggled to reflect his personality. The book appears in an election year, a timing of obvious risk for John Key. When I sought his co-operation it was on the understanding that this would not be an 'authorised' biography. At no stage was he offered, nor did he seek, an opportunity to see the finished text or any part of it before publication. All unattributed views and conclusions are mine.

John Roughan
May 2014

Introduction

On a summer's evening shortly after New Year 2014, New Zealand television news channels carried a tantalising glimpse of the country's Prime Minister, holidaying in Hawaii, playing golf with the President of the United States. In polo shirt and shorts, John Key watched his son Max sink a putt and receive a high-five from Barack Obama. New Zealand's diplomats were agog. This was face time beyond their dreams. How had it happened?

The invitation, Key explains, had been made a month earlier at the funeral of Nelson Mandela. He was sitting with Australia's new Prime Minister, Tony Abbott, when Obama came into view. Abbott asked Key to introduce them. As the three of them chatted, Obama said to Key, 'You going to Hawaii this year?'

'Yes,' said Key.

'We should play golf,' suggested the President.

Key agreed.

Obama indicated he was serious, inviting Key to have 'your people' talk to his personal aide, Marvin Nicholson.

Back in Wellington, Key's chief of staff Wayne Eagleson and foreign affairs adviser Ben King kept the invitation to themselves as they made the arrangements. It was not their place to disclose what the US President might do on vacation. They were not even sure if they would be allowed to tell anybody afterwards. They let the New Zealand foreign ministry know only a day or two beforehand. After all, it might not happen. Any number of unexpected events could cause the White House to cancel a game of golf.

Barring an incident, Key was confident it would happen. He knew the offer was genuine, that it wasn't merely one of those 'We must catch up sometime' gestures. But he had not even told his son that he was invited too. Max, who had finished his first year at university, was staying in Auckland for New Year and due to arrive in Hawaii a day too late for the game. When his father called to say, 'If you want to get here a day earlier you can play golf with Barack Obama', Max was on the next plane.

Obama chose a course on a military base 20 kilometres from Honolulu and not far from his Oahu holiday home. The Keys – whose Hawaiian retreat is on Maui – had to island-hop. Once they were out on the course, small groups of military families gathered at every vantage point to see the President. During the game, Obama would walk over, shake their hands and thank them for their service. Key's people need not have worried about publicity. A White House photographer accompanied the players for the entire 18 holes and media were waiting at the second hole.

That is how it happened, but Key's unassuming account does not go to the heart of why these things happen for him. In between strokes, he and Obama talked about their work and families and lives. Key mentioned that he, wife Bronagh, daughter Stephie and son Max had been guests of the Queen at Balmoral Castle the previous year. Obama thought he meant an invitation to dinner. 'No,' explained Key, 'we went for the weekend.' He talks more about that weekend than royal protocol may permit, though the Queen might not be surprised. It was not protocol that prompted her invitation – she is not obliged to entertain prime ministers at her private estate for a weekend. So, how does Key explain that one?

> To this day, I don't know why, but she invited us. It was a long time ago, before the Christchurch earthquake, and her private secretary came up to me after an audience and said, 'Her Majesty wonders if you would like to come to Balmoral?' I said, 'Yes, that'd be great.' So they formally invited us, but the Christchurch earthquake postponed that, which she understood. The next time I was there, the Queen asked after the family and I mentioned that Stephie was over from Paris. The Queen said, 'You should bring her to see me.' So I did, and on the way out the private secretary said to me, 'The Queen thinks you should bring your whole family to Balmoral.'

It was arranged for the third weekend of September 2013. William and Catherine and the baby would be there with several friends. Britain's Prime Minister David Cameron was coming for the Sunday night. John and Bronagh with Stephie and Max arrived on the Friday evening and were shown to rooms inside the castle.

> They are not overly flash. I mean, it's a castle. They

haven't spent enormous money to make it lavish. It's lovely. It's warm, though they can't stay there in winter – it's too big to heat. There are no showers; you take baths. It is incredibly relaxed. There's obviously a degree of formality insomuch that if the Queen goes to leave the room, everyone stands. But outside of that it is extremely informal.

They knew one of the evening meals would be a barbecue and the other a black-tie dinner, but did not know which it was on the night they arrived. 'It doesn't matter to me,' laughs Key, 'I can put a black tie on in two minutes. They had spring-loaded cufflinks there for dressing really fast.' That night it was the barbecue, held somewhere on the estate. John and Bronagh went in the Queen's Range Rover, the Queen driving with a corgi on the seat beside her. William drove the car behind with Stephie and Max. Prince Philip had gone ahead to oversee the setting-up.

The barbecue was in a small house with a long table. The Queen, wearing a sweater and kilt, set out the plates. At one point in the evening, Key, sitting next to her, saw his daughter in fits of laughter with William about something, his son at the other end of the table talking to Kate, and thought, 'This is quite surreal.'

In a lot of ways, I'm used to seeing famous people. I go to lots of meetings and over time I have got more used to it. But it was the fact that the family were there. It was the same with playing golf with Obama. It was great, but it was really cool that Max was playing with him. There's lots of things the family give up [for my career] and the really nice thing is they will have some incredible memories one day when they look back, hopefully.

The next morning, William and friends took Max grouse-shooting and Catherine invited Stephie on a long walk. They all got back in time for the Queen to take them on a tour of the estate before a picnic.

> She took us to places you can't get to on a tour – a lot of them have to do with Queen Victoria. She just loves Victoria, and she loves Balmoral. It's a bit like us going to Hawaii. It's the only place she can drive herself and be a bit more normal, [where] she has some freedom. She drove us a way up to quite a cold part of the estate and we were having the picnic when this guy comes out of nowhere, a hiker – the United Kingdom has a right to roam, you can go anywhere – and the Queen walked over to him, said, 'Hello, how are you?', and he told her he was planning to walk some place. She pointed out to him where it was and he wandered off.

The striking thing about these anecdotes is that they are told with an attitude neither of awe nor cynicism. They suggest Key treats the great and famous much as he treats most people – with genuine interest. Probably the reason he receives these invitations is simply that those issuing them like him and find him good company. It is easy to like someone who gives almost everyone he meets his full attention, without prejudice or effort, and possesses the invaluable political attribute of remembering a name after a single introduction months, even years, before.

Being likeable, though, does not completely explain the qualities that have made John Key so successful in politics thus far. He has a keen instinct for what matters to most people and, just as important, what does not matter.

Within a year of coming to office, commentators were calling him a 'phenomenon'. Yet he is not a great speaker, not an imposing figure, and his face offers cartoonists no distinctive features for their purpose. He is not one of those leaders with a 'presence' that makes everyone in a crowded room instantly aware when he enters.

He looks and sounds ordinary, though, equally obviously, he is not. He has an air of calm self-assurance that, thanks to his manner, does not come across as superior. Yet his career in finance took him to a higher position in the world than anyone who has previously brought business credentials to New Zealand politics. He makes little reference in speeches and interviews to the heights he attained in currency trading, regularly commuting between the world's financial capitals, London and New York, working almost every other week in Wall Street.

Precious few top-flight business leaders can be enticed into politics. They shudder at the idea of what must be done to win the right to govern a country: the intemperate public debates, personal criticism, door-knocking, instant answers to complicated problems, the whole contrived courtship of news media that dimly understand business and seem to resent its capacity to create wealth. John Key needed no enticing; politics has attracted him since his youth.

The boy in this book, growing up in a poor neighbour-hood surrounded by the better-off, and inspired by a hard-working solo mother, did not have the usual up-bringing of a future National Party leader. His years in high school gave teachers no hint of what he would later achieve, and he went to university for a ticket to business, not the social and philosophical subjects that normally interest a budding politician – not even economics. Key is not a reflective man, given to dwelling on his own past, or that of the country he governs. He is attuned to the present, trusting the instincts that served him richly in foreign exchange markets and safely so far in government. He has a currency dealer's sure sense of the mood and movement of the market at the moment, although he is less sure in his long view. He is passing to a future government the projected health costs and pensions of an ageing population, and an economy still with a narrow trading base, excessive property investment and declining home ownership among the young.

New Zealand's recent history holds little resonance for Key. When he went to the Mandela funeral he took along none of those in New Zealand who were in the long campaign to stop the country playing rugby against white South Africa. At the funeral he enjoyed a conversation with the rock star Bono and was surprised to learn how large a concern apartheid had been for someone growing up in Ireland. Key is honest that the subject was not much on his mind at the same age. More surprisingly, since his priorities are economic, he never acknowledges the work of those in previous governments who took unpopular decisions to bequeath him a market-led economy with sound public accounts.

It is a theme of this book that history matters for lessons that need to be remembered. But the past is less important than the present and the future is made by what a government does today. John Key's life to date has been remarkable and his politics are important for New Zealand's future. In the following pages we will trace the experiences that have shaped him, and meet people close to him, including Bronagh with her quiet sense of humour. We will go inside his government and hear how it works, operating a closer partnership with supporting parties than the previous government. Ultimately, this account will offer a view on what Key is doing with his lease of power and where he is taking New Zealand.

CHAPTER ONE

Broken Home

The boy was just six years old – too young to remember what was happening to him that fateful night. His sister was a little older. She remembers their mother rousing them from sleep and getting them dressed to leave. Their father was not in the house. Their mother and older sister had packed the family car and were ready to go. They drove away that night, a woman in her mid-forties with a teenaged daughter and two children at primary school. The children never saw their father again.

The boy, John Key, and his sister, Sue, had been happy living on Auckland's beautiful waterfront at St Heliers. The beach was just across the road from their house at the back of a restaurant their parents had bought. Sue remembers swimming nearly every day when they came home from school in the long golden summers of an Auckland childhood. John fondly recalls them exploring the little bush reserve at St Heliers called Dingle Dell, and remembers the beach on one day in particular when a storm blew in and he convinced his mother to let him go swimming. The thrill of the waves crashing upon him lives with him still.

But inside the house, life was not so happy. George Key, a middle-aged Englishman, had not settled easily in New Zealand. His wife, Ruth, eight years younger, found it much easier. Ruth had escaped Nazi-occupied Austria with her mother and brother on the eve of World War II and she had learned in London how to make a new life. Her well-to-do Jewish family had owned a good business in Vienna until they had to leave with nothing. George's parents, too, had run a successful business, selling pharmaceutical supplies and owning shops in Portsmouth. George was working in the firm when Ruth went to stay with them there after the war. But George was never to be as successful in business for himself.

He and Ruth were married in 1948 and had their first child, Elizabeth, the following year. In 1955 they emigrated to New Zealand. Their ship had been destined for Wellington but Elizabeth had caught measles on board and they were quarantined at its next port of call, Sydney. Liz Cave (née Key) laughs about it now because measles are contagious only before the spots appear. When eventually they were allowed to leave, it was on a ship heading for Auckland.

George was an Englishman of his time. Well-read and well-spoken, he never exchanged his long trousers for the shorts that most Kiwi men wear in summer. The family had settled in the warm far north of New Zealand, in the idyllic Bay of Islands, where they rented a house at the small port of Opua. George found work as a health tester for cow herds on the surrounding farms and was happy in the job, as Liz remembers. She doesn't know why her father eventually gave up the outdoor work for a job in the laundry at the Moerewa freezing works.

Ruth, meanwhile, was a receptionist at the hospital in nearby Kawakawa. When she was hired, they had been anxious to know whether she intended to have more children – too many staff had recently left to have babies. A month after she started, Ruth became pregnant. Sue was born at the hospital in 1958. With two daughters, Ruth was fervently hoping her next child would be a son. 'Mum was a typical Jewish mother,' laughs Sue many years later, 'a son was everything to her. She often told Liz and me that if her third baby had been another girl she'd have carried right on trying until she got a boy.'

John Phillip Key arrived on 9 August 1961. By then the family had moved to Auckland where their address, coincidentally, was 9 August Place, a quiet cul-de-sac near One Tree Hill. The future Prime Minister came to regard the coincidence of the date and place as a happy omen, although, like other homes of his Auckland childhood, he has had no interest in revisiting it. If he did, he would find he could claim to have been born in a stable. His family had one of a cluster of stucco units that used to be stables for horses kept by the August family before the estate was subdivided sometime after World War II. During the war, American servicemen from the nearby barracks that later became Cornwall Hospital used to come and ride the horses for recreation. According to the current owner of the units, now named The Stables, there are still iron tethers behind the wall linings.

In Auckland, George had found work in a plastics factory and Ruth with a milliner across the street from their first home in the city at 50 Great South Road, now a car yard. Keen to work for themselves, they bought a contract to run the works cafeteria at the Auckland milk treatment plant at Penrose. By that time they had moved to Campbell Road and John had started primary school, joining Sue at Cornwall Park District School. George and Ruth worked all the hours they could. Sue remembers going to the treatment plant on a Christmas Day because they were working. The young family had no relatives in New Zealand. There were no wider family gatherings to attend unless George's parents were visiting from England, which they did five times in 10 years after George and Ruth emigrated.

George was into his fifties and Ruth in her forties when they bought the restaurant at St Heliers. It was at the end of the last block of shops on Tamaki Drive before the road leaves the waterfront and winds uphill. They called the restaurant Harbour Lights. Dining out was still rare in New Zealand in the mid-1960s. Men might go for a beer together after work, but by law pubs had to close at 6 p.m. Women, who were not yet in the workforce in large numbers, would be at home preparing an evening meal, often for husbands who returned the worse for wear after rapidly downing jugs in the 'six o'clock swill' before closing time. Restrictive laws had a perverse effect, as they often do. When last orders were called, many of the patrons had half-gallon 'jars' filled from the bar and took them home, or elsewhere, to drink through the evening.

Fortunately, change was coming – six o'clock closing was abolished after a referendum in October 1967 – but a wine and dining culture was still some years away. Liz, who worked with her parents in the Harbour Lights, served the basic dishes of the day – steak and chips and even 'boil in the bag' meals that she shudders to recall. They mainly did lunches and some late-afternoon servings. She doesn't remember the restaurant being open at nights. It was a struggle, but that was not the only problem. George was drinking.

He had come from a family that enjoyed a drink, and he was probably a heavy drinker before the restaurant started to accumulate debts. But now it was worse, particularly for Ruth who didn't drink. Looking back, Liz believes her father felt isolated in New Zealand. 'As an Englishman, in the way he spoke and dressed, he would have been different, particularly at that time. Mum loved New Zealand but Dad never really fitted in. Drink became his escape.'

George had been well educated. He spoke five languages including German, Ruth's native tongue, although they conversed in English – Ruth with a guttural Austrian accent. George had served in the war where his multilingual skills could have been put to use in intelligence, but if so, he kept his military record to himself. Liz, Sue and John have no idea what he did. He had a previous marriage that had not survived the war. In later years Ruth told John that George's parents used to send him money in New Zealand. 'He hadn't had to work much, that's the way Mum used to see it,' Key explains. 'He had drifted along, did all kinds of things, and had businesses that fell over. He had never had to perform, as Mum saw it, and she was the opposite, very driven and focused.'

Their rows were frequent and terrible, according to Sue. There was one in particular that John Key has never forgotten. It happened one night when his father came home later than he should have. He had been drinking and had bought a toy for his son – an electronic car circuit perhaps; John cannot remember. All that he does remember is that his mother erupted in fury and as a boy he couldn't understand why.

There came a point when she could take no more. When she roused the children from their beds that night and asked Liz to take them all away, Ruth not only wanted to leave George, she wanted to leave Auckland, get right away, make yet another new start in her life somewhere else. They headed south. Liz had barely driven beyond Auckland before and her mother, who couldn't drive, wanted to go all the way to Wellington. They stayed overnight along the way and arrived in Wellington where they immediately began to realise how hard life was now going to be. They looked for accommodation and were shown places they might afford – vile places, Liz recalls, flats that still had outside lavatories.

They did not stay long in the capital where John would one day make his name. They went to a smaller town, Havelock North in Hawke's Bay, where they spent some time in a caravan, Sue remembers, and she and John attended the local primary school. After a period in Havelock North, they moved on again, this time heading to the South Island, to Christchurch. They drove to Wellington and bought berths on the interisland ferry. As the ship sailed out towards Cook Strait, they passed the *Wahine* lying on its side where it had sunk after hitting a reef in a blinding storm on 10 April that year, 1968.

In Christchurch, they rented a house in Glade Avenue, Richmond, near the Avon River and not far from the city centre. Ruth got a job as a night porter in the city's prestigious Clarendon Hotel where the Queen stayed on royal visits and the Beatles had been pictured waving to the crowds from its balcony during their tour four years earlier. Liz found work at the Opawa supermarket. Sue and John attended Richmond Primary School. Today, those streets of eastern Christchurch near the river have been largely abandoned, 'red-zoned', the land having slipped towards the river in the devastating earthquakes of September 2010 and February 2011. The Clarendon, too, was demolished along with most of the inner city's grand old buildings as a result of damage sustained in the second quake. But at Glade Avenue in 1969, Ruth Key and her children were getting settled at last. They had got to know the neighbours. John remembers the woman next door had blackcurrant bushes and one day invited Ruth to send the kids over to pick the fruit.

> We did that and Mum made jam with it. She gave us a jar to take to the little old lady, and on the way over, Sue dropped the thing. So we went home, got an empty jar and scooped up all the jam, probably with glass in it, and gave it to the lady. Fortunately, Sue soon 'fessed up and Mum went straight across to replace it.

Liz was aware that since leaving Auckland, Ruth had been getting letters from George, trying to convince her to return. Sue, too, received letters from him and has kept some of them. One day in May, a policeman came to their door. In Auckland, George had died. Heavy drinking had probably caused the coronary artery disease and acute congestive heart failure disclosed by a post-mortem. People who saw him would not have known he had a problem, says Liz. 'It wasn't apparent in public. He never had hangovers or anything – 99.9 per cent of people around him would have had no idea.' John, seven years old by then, remembers asking his mother if he should go to the funeral. She told him it wouldn't be necessary. If he was told anything about the service and the burial he has forgotten it. When interviewed for this book he believed his father's grave was somewhere in Auckland but had no idea where.

New Zealand's registry of deaths records that George Ernest Key died aged 55 on 14 May 1969 and was buried eight days later in a soldiers' plot at Waikumete Cemetery. His last address was in Esplanade Road, Mt Eden. The death certificate lists no occupation.

Talking of their father now, Liz and Sue describe a highly intelligent but distant man and an avid reader: 'He read everything that was available.' Liz remembers Ruth going to the library and bringing him about five books a week. 'I don't know why he didn't go himself. I don't recall Mum reading very much.' Physically, he looked 'not unlike John does today [at 52], except he was bald.' George did not relate easily to children. Sue recalls that he once took them to the Auckland Museum. Photographs survive of Sue and John with their mother at Rotorua, the children in matching hand-knitted jerseys with the Fair Isle pattern common at the time. The snaps were probably taken by George. It was a rare holiday, probably their last before the break-up. Sue wonders if it was a final attempt to save their marriage. John Key knows only what his mother has told him about his father, usually as a lesson in life for him.

> For example, she used to say to me, 'There are "doers" and "payers" [those who can do things and those who pay other people to do them]. Your father was a payer and I think you will be too, so you had better get a decent education.' He was absolutely useless at making or fixing things and I am the same, absolutely bloody useless.

Ruth told John not much else. 'Occasionally, I'd ask her

about Dad and she wouldn't talk about it. That was how Mum was. She never talked about the war or anything like that.' Growing up, he knew there was a picture of his father in a drawer in the house and he took it out just to look at it. He felt the absence sometimes when he was playing junior rugby and his mother would come to watch him. Not many women were on the sidelines of rugby fields in those days.

There was one occasion in particular when he wished he still had a father. Sex education specialists, usually women, used to visit Christchurch schools to give talks segregated as 'father and son' and 'mother and daughter' evenings. John went to the father-and-son session with his best friend Gary Donnelly and Gary's father, a policeman. It was not until the talks began that fathers and sons realised how intimate, frank and graphic the material would be. It was not what you wanted to hear with a man who is not your dad.

> I remember odd things like that, but for the most part it was okay. [As Prime Minister] I see lots of kids who have lost their fathers – in Afghanistan, for example – and I've seen them later. Kids are remarkable at coping with situations. What's around you is what you think is normal.

The day after Ruth received word of George's death she received another official notice. He had left her with debts from their Auckland restaurant. Liz believes the amount was a couple of thousand, which would be the equivalent of more than $40,000 today. New Zealand's average weekly wage in 1969 was just under $50. Ruth went to an accountant and learned that she had the option of declaring bankruptcy or trying to pay the debt off. A combination of fierce pride and a fear of bankruptcy left her no option. She resolved to pay it off as soon as she could. Her prospects of doing so became a little better thanks to another consequence of her husband's death. As a widow, Ruth now qualified for a state house.

CHAPTER TWO

Poor Boy?

Many times in his life when he has landed at
Christchurch Airport and driven into the city,
John Key has taken a short detour, turning
from Memorial Avenue at Greers Road and driving past
his old school, Burnside High, then past Jellie Park with
its plaza of swimming pools where his bike was once
stolen. It was a 'chopper' with a banana seat and ape-
hanger handlebars. Turning right into Clyde Road he is in
the neighbourhood he knew. Hollyford Avenue is on the
left. At a bend in the street, set well back on an unfenced
mown lawn, sits a modest, tidy, white wood and fibro
house. A crude carport on one side could be the same one
he helped to build when he was 10. It is a street of similar
houses, better or worse for wear. Some bear the signs of
dispirited poverty: torn curtains in dusty windows, uncut
grass, run-down cars in the yard, old containers and other
household detritus lying about. Most are not like that –
they are the homes of people with not much to spend on

furnishings but caring for their appearance, making the best of what they have been given.

A low-rent state house was like winning a lottery for a widow with young children and little income. Ruth Key was doubly lucky to be given a house in a small pocket of state housing in the fairly well-off northwestern suburbs of Christchurch. The relative poverty of Hollyford Avenue, Hooker Avenue and Earnslaw Crescent might be at odds with the alpine attractions they were named for, but it was a neighbourhood where a poor boy with a paper round biked no further than a few blocks before he noticed how other people lived, a place where a determined mother could let her children know that, although she had come down in the world, a better life was within their reach.

Today the area is leafy with trees and hedges that were low shrubs when Ruth arrived in 1969 with Liz (19), Sue (10) and John (8). Liz was earning a wage and Ruth was working nights at the Clarendon to try to pay off the Auckland debts. John remembers a jar in the house where his mother saved all her tips. Household finances were tight. Ruth budgeted with envelopes marked for rent, power and other bills, and she would not raid them for anything. 'If there was no money for a present or something,' recalls Sue, 'there was no money. It stayed in the envelopes. That was it.' She remembers upsetting her mother once, probably before she got the state house.

> I remember we were having chicken for dinner and I was looking everywhere for some salt. I finally asked Mum and I remember she started crying because she couldn't afford it that week. I remember because that was the only time I saw her cry. She was pretty strong. You learned not to ask for things, because why would

you upset her? Even as a child you soon learned she was doing her damndest.

Liz was proud of her younger siblings as well as her mother. 'She was good to her children and they were good to her.' John, though, does not want to overstate their poverty.

> We didn't feel poor. I know economically we were, but there were never these ridiculous stories you hear about kids getting saveloy water for dinner. There was enough food. Mum wasn't the greatest cook in the world, though I liked it when I was a kid. She'd cook Wiener schnitzel and roast chicken and things. We wouldn't go on lavish holidays or anything. There weren't big presents. But we had clothes, we could go to movies. We did all the things normal kids did.

Their home was small but warm, dry, neat and clean. Ruth was a fastidious housekeeper. They had three bedrooms and a narrow hall opening onto a tight kitchen and an adjoining living room where she had bright-orange cushions on the vinyl couches. In his bedroom John had a crystal radio set and a desk as well as a chest of drawers and a single bed with a bright-orange bedspread.

> We had hot-water bottles in winter and we always had baths on Sunday nights when she'd wash our hair with vinegar: we wanted her to – it tasted good. She'd use shampoo and then vinegar and water. And then there was this crazy thing she did: she had a lolly jar and if you brushed your teeth properly you could have two lollies from the jar – *after* you'd brushed your teeth!

Her job at the hotel in the city meant Ruth had to leave the children in Liz's care overnight, but she could finish her shift at the Clarendon in time to get home on a morning bus, give them breakfast and see them off to school – John to Aorangi Primary where they gave him free stationery, which he happily reported to his new classmates who were not so lucky. (Fifty years later, Aorangi School was closed by the Key government.) As soon as the house was empty and tidy, Ruth could get some sleep. She was usually up again before Sue and John got home and there was time for an evening meal together before she had to leave for work.

Liz left home at the end of 1969 to travel to England on the ship *Oriana*. Their grandfather, George's father, had died in 1967 and their grandmother was not expected to live long. John vividly remembers Liz's departure because the *Oriana* had soft drinks in cans. He had never seen drinks in cans before. That was New Zealand in 1969 – a protected economy with largely locally manufactured consumer goods. International trends were slow to be adopted and travellers returned with luggage trundlers full of overseas purchases that were either not available or not as cheap in New Zealand. From England, Liz used to send her little brother presents of magic kits. She was away for three years but her departure would not have made much more room in the house. Ruth also had a succession of boarders – 'all young men who hadn't really wanted to leave home', as Liz described them. 'She looked after them very well.'

Evening meals were a lively event in Ruth's house. Invariably she would raise a subject for debate and every-one around the table was expected to have an opinion on it. 'No opinion was wrong,' Sue explains, 'but you couldn't *not* have an opinion.' There was no shortage of issues in the early 1970s. The Vietnam War was dragging on, rugby tours with South Africa were bringing mass mobilisations of protest in the streets of Christchurch, environmentalism had arrived, feminism was just getting started.

National was in government and Sir Keith Holyoake was still Prime Minister, but the politician who provoked most discussion everywhere in New Zealand at that time was the Minister of Finance and certain future leader, Rob Muldoon. Pugnacious and clever, Muldoon courted controversy and intimidated critics with a malicious wit. New Zealanders admired him or detested him in equal measure, but few were indifferent. 'Mum adamantly didn't like Muldoon,' Sue recalls. John did.

> I kind of admired him because he seemed a strong leader who was in control and stood up to stuff. [Like TV interviewers?] Yes, there was a bit of that that I kinda liked. But he was a completely different style of person to me, [a] completely different character. Modern-day politics is different too.

The subject Ruth brought to the table was usually something she had read in the paper – a hotel night porter could probably pick one up at work and have plenty of time to read it in the small hours. Ruth may have also had spare moments when she could catch a television programme on politics and current affairs. It was the great age of the television political interview. Current affairs programmes with strongly opinionated interrogators such as Brian Edwards and David Beatson would invite politicians into their studio for a ritual slaying. Only one politician of the time invariably got the better of them: Muldoon.

Ruth and her young son thrived on their dinner-table debates. 'Mum was always very left,' says Sue. 'I think she felt she had been shafted by the whole system; and John was never left, right from the beginning, so they argued until the cows came home.' On reflection she adds, 'Probably she wasn't as left as she made out, but the more that John was right, the more left she went.' John thinks 'a lot of it was just to make me think'.

> She was Labour but she wasn't a political person really. She was in a state house on the widow's benefit, she would have voted Labour, but if I sat down with her today I'm pretty sure I could convince her that what we are doing now is right. She didn't like Muldoon – she thought he was a bully. I think he reminded her of her past.

It was around 1970–71, when he was just nine or 10, that John Key started telling the family he was determined to do two things in life: make a million dollars and become Prime Minister of New Zealand. 'Those were his two burning desires,' Sue says, 'to make a million dollars, then to be Prime Minister. It was always in that order. Mum, being Mum, said, "Of course you can." Mum never put you down.'

Ruth's allegiance remained with Labour, particularly when Norman Kirk came to power in 1972, but she had no illusions about which side of politics would engage her son. When Kirk died in 1974, Liz and Sue went to his lying in state in the Christchurch Town Hall. John, just turned 13, was not there, though some time later he wrote to Kirk's successor, Bill Rowling, asking what he should do to become Prime Minister. Rowling wrote back but none of the family has kept the letter. It was the following year, when Muldoon was coming in, that John mischievously presented his mother with a National Party rosette. He assumed she would throw it away, but at her death 25 years later the family found it among her treasures.

––––––––––

John Key's first aim in life – to make a million dollars – is easy to understand given his circumstances. The only time he can recall upsetting his mother was in one of the dinner-table debates when the subject was money and he said to her, 'We have nothing. I want more than nothing.' She became tearful and said to him, 'That's not quite fair.' He regretted it immediately. 'I backed off really quickly and never went there again. It was the only time I can remember saying something like that.'

They had a lot more than nothing. Ruth sewed and darned and knitted their clothes. Though they were renting the house, they painted it when necessary. John kept the lawns mowed. 'Mum used to say that just because you're poor you don't have to have bad standards. She was fiercely determined.'

Like many of her generation, including her late husband, she had been a long-time smoker. John was 11 or 12, a pupil at Cobham Intermediate School, when he started telling her to stop. 'You've got to be around because I don't have anyone else,' he'd tell her. Sue, too, hated the smell of smoke in the house. It didn't help that her mother, unlike the parents of all her secretly smoking friends at high school, did not mind if Sue smoked, though Sue never did. 'Because we were allowed to, we didn't bother. Mum was very much in that mode: you could do what you wanted and if you were letting anyone down it was yourself.' It took another four or five years of John's exhortation but one day

Ruth announced she was going to use acupuncture to help her give up. To John's relief, 'she came home next day and never smoked again'.

When Ruth had paid off the debts she gave up her hotel night work to become a house cleaner. Many of her jobs were in nearby Fendalton. One of her clients, a doctor and his wife, had a beautiful house, as John describes it, with a swimming pool. They used to invite Ruth to bring her son around and in school holidays he would swim in the pool while she was cleaning. John's paper round also took him into part of Fendalton. He delivered the Christchurch *Star* every afternoon after school and went around collecting the money on Saturdays. Observing the houses of the better-off, he thought, 'That's where I want to be.'

One day, while still at Cobham Intermediate, he came home and announced he was going to learn to play golf. It seemed to be an occupational necessity if he was going to be a businessman. Sue remembers Ruth's reaction: 'Mum looked at him like, "Hello, we're still in a state house, John. How are we going to afford golf lessons? Get real."' But he found the money for lessons, probably from the paper round and picking raspberries in summer holidays, as thousands of Christchurch teenagers used to do before the city's western spread covered the orchards.

John was not, by all accounts, a natural sportsman, though he was keen. He and his mother shared a love of rugby, which was another frequent topic at the dinner table. He played halfback in junior teams for the Burnside rugby club and his hero was Sid Going. 'John would have given his eye teeth to be Sid Going,' says Sue. One of their early lodgers, 24-year-old Roger Norton, was playing rugby for Burnside's top team when he first lived with the Keys. When he went out for a jog, 10-year-old John wanted to tag along. Not at first, though, says Norton. 'He was a wee bit reserved towards me at the start.' When the boy became more at ease, they also played table tennis in the kitchen where there was hardly room to swing a bat. 'He wasn't a great ball player,' Norton remembers, but he was keen to learn. 'John was a bright boy, always interested in everything. He was always inquiring of his mother, asked his mother a lot of things.' Norton, who still has a mischievous sense of humour, knew of John's ambitions and remembers a time when he teased his mother with it.

> We were on the back lawn at Hollyford Ave and politics came up. As soon as Ruth talked politics I knew how to rumble her a bit. Ruth hated Muldoon, absolutely hated him. John was there and I remember this day I grabbed him, pinched his cheek like Muldoon's and said, 'Guess who's going to be Prime Minister one day?' Ruth said, 'You mark my words, Roger, John *will* be Prime Minister one day', and I said, 'Bullshit!' Boy, have I eaten humble pie.

Ruth did not quite live long enough to see her prediction come to pass. But she, more than anyone, had shaped the values, self-confidence and personality of the future Prime Minister. Although she never talked very much about her life before the war, or the Holocaust, the following chapter reveals a little more of what happened to her family and of Ruth's own remarkable life.

CHAPTER THREE

Ruth

Ruth Lazar spent her childhood and early teens in a comfortably wealthy Jewish household in Vienna with her father Max, her mother Margarethe (Greta) and her older brother Herbert. From the little that Ruth said later about her upbringing, her daughters deduced that she was attended by maids, a cook and a tutor. She was home-schooled. Her father owned and managed a leather company in partnership with his brothers, Jacques and Norbert. The firm of Simmeringer Lederwerke Gebrüder Lazar did industrial leather tanning, dyeing and finishing, but its core business was trading, particularly in fine leathers.

Ruth was 14 years old in 1936 when her father died of leukaemia at 53. Her uncle Jacques took over the management of the business but ominous clouds were gathering over Austria. Across the border in Germany, Hitler had come to power. One of the Nazi government's first acts had been to urge Germans to boycott Jewish businesses and professions. Many had been shut down and Jewish doctors and lawyers were no longer permitted to practise there. The first concentration camps had been established. Hitler was rearming Germany to avenge its defeat in World War I and fulfil his fantasy of a new and ethnically pure German empire: a 'Third Reich' excluding Jews. There was little doubt Austria would be his first target.

Hitler's armies crossed the border unopposed in March 1938. Jacques Lazar had already scaled back the company to concentrate on wholesaling, a business with less need of a public profile. After the Nazi takeover, life soon became untenable for Austrian Jews. They were being told to leave, and those who could sell their property and had somewhere to go were going. Through 1938, Jacques and Norbert tried unsuccessfully to wind up the company. In November, during anti-Semitic riots in Vienna, the authorities closed the Lazars' business. Jacques and Norbert were taken into 'protective custody' and sent to Dachau concentration camp near Munich. They were released on condition they leave the Reich.

Fatally but naturally, the brothers resumed their attempt to wind up the business, hoping to settle its tax bills and debts, particularly to 'Aryan' creditors. They hoped to have enough left to emigrate with some means of starting anew. However, in February 1939 the company was confiscated and put in the hands of a liquidator, aptly named Ernst Muck, a Nazi Party member who turned out to be a crook. While Jacques and Norbert waited fruitlessly for their money from the liquidation, Ruth's mother decided it was time for her and her children to get out.

They owe their lives to her mother's sister, Charlotte ('Lottie') Karpeles, a stunningly beautiful woman even late in life when she visited the Keys in New Zealand.

Lottie had met and married an English soldier for the sole purpose of finding a refuge. The family believes she never saw the soldier again after the marriage of convenience. Lottie ensured that Greta, Herbert and Ruth got to London sometime before Britain declared war in September 1939. Their departure must have been dangerous, for they travelled light. Ruth later said they had walked a long way. Her daughter Liz treasures a small tapestry that came from a chair in the house in Vienna, possibly pocketed by Ruth as they fled. 'It is probably the only thing she was able to take – no photograph albums, nothing except a tapestry.' Liz has had it framed. 'It is very pretty but quite sad.'

In London, aged 16, Ruth's first need was to learn English, which she did, and went to work with Lottie, a milliner in an age when hats were universally worn outdoors. Lottie, as Charlotte Weiss, later became a successful London designer showing two collections a year. During the war Ruth also signed up with the British Army's Auxiliary Territorial Service where women volunteers worked as clerks, cooks and telephonists. She would not have been a cook. According to her daughter Sue, Ruth was never much of a cook because all her meals had been prepared for her when she was growing up. 'She told us, "I had maids, I never did anything." John, Liz and I can all cook well – John cooks very well – because Mum was not so good.'

If Ruth in wartime had any idea what was happening to the Lazars left in Vienna, she did not talk about it in later life. Their fate was made known to the Key family as recently as 2010 when New Zealand's Minister of Foreign Affairs Murray McCully told the Federal President of Austria, Dr Heinz Fischer, that the Prime Minister's mother had been a refugee from the Nazi occupation. A dossier that Fischer arranged to have compiled from war records is chilling to read.

Although under constant pressure to leave, Jacques and Norbert remained in Vienna through 1940, awaiting some funds from the sale of a building and other property of their confiscated company. Its assets had been valued as high as 104,000 reichsmarks. The liquidator, Muck, agreed to sell to a cinema-owning couple, fellow Nazi Party members, for 60,000 reichsmarks. Once Muck deducted his costs and various other expenses, there was just 45,400 left for the Lazars. They never received it. Muck was eventually investigated and replaced as liquidator in May 1941, but the money could not be found. By then it was too late anyway. The dossier states:

> As a result of the embezzlement of the proceeds from the liquidation of the company, Jacques and Norbert Lazar were unable to raise in time the money needed for their emigration. On 15 February, 1941, Jacques and Norbert Lazar and Norbert's wife Mathilde were deported on the first deportation train from Vienna to the ghetto in Opole, a small town near Lublin in the German Occupied General Government of Poland. From early 1942 this ghetto was 'liquidated' and the inhabitants deported to the extermination camps Belzec and Sobibor. The Lazars were declared dead after 1945.

The document continues:

> Max Lazar had another brother, Leo Lazar, born 13 April, 1890 [married to Irma, née Wodak, born 20 July 1889], who was, however, not involved in the family business but instead worked as a 'remisier' [stockbroker].

Leo and his wife Irma Lazar managed to flee to France but were caught there by the Nazi authorities and on 23 June, 1943, deported from the Drancy assembly camp (northeast of Paris) to Auschwitz.

It goes on to record that Leo and Irma had two daughters who survived the Holocaust, as did Norbert and Mathilde's daughter Herta. She, like Ruth's immediate family, had escaped to England.

At home with his mother, John Key would sometimes notice her start to cry if a programme involving Hitler's concentration camps came on TV. 'I'd ask her about it and she'd just say, "I don't want to talk about it." She hated the Germans, eh. For a long, long time she was really bitter about all the things that happened. Well, not the Germans, the Nazis.' Nevertheless, Key appears to have less curiosity about his Jewish roots than his sisters, who at different times have both travelled to Vienna to try to learn something of their mother's heritage. When his elder sister Liz went back to England in 1969, only Lottie was still alive. Ruth's mother Greta had died in 1958 and her brother Herbert is said to have been killed shortly after the war when attempting to enter Palestine before the creation of Israel.

Living in London in the early seventies, Liz started attending a synagogue, as she had done with her mother when they lived in Auckland. Ruth had stopped attending since coming to Christchurch and she sent John to a Christian Sunday school at St Aidan's Anglican Church. When Liz returned from Britain, in time for Ruth's fiftieth birthday in November 1972, she took her mother to the Christchurch synagogue, then in Gloucester Street. According to her sister, 'Liz was distraught because she discovered she was more orthodox than the jolly rabbi there.'

Ruth did not return to the religion of her birth until she was in her sixties and then it was with a practical mission. 'Mum did a huge amount of work before she died,' says Sue, 'trying to free up a lot of money sitting in New York for [Jewish] war victims. She spent countless hours working at the synagogue trying to free up that money for other people.' Ruth and other heirs of the Lazar brothers' confiscated property had received payments from a German restitution fund since the early 1960s.

Ruth Key instilled in her children the practical secular values of education and hard work, along with a conviction that they were not meant to be living in their present situation. 'Mum made that quite clear to us,' says Sue. 'We were there by a wrong turn, a freak of nature. If the war hadn't come along she wouldn't have been poor. By the grace of stuff that happened, we ended up in a situation we should never have been in and we were damned sure we weren't staying there.'

With her menial earnings, a widow's benefit and an Austrian war pension, Ruth was able to pay off all the debts by about 1973. The following year she could afford to take Sue (16) and John (13) to Sydney at Christmas. It was their first trip on a plane. She remained living at Hollyford Avenue where there were good schools nearby. From Cobham Intermediate, John was going on to Burnside High School.

John's education, his sisters knew, came first. 'Mum wanted John to go to university,' says Sue. 'I wanted to go too but Mum couldn't afford for both of us to go, so the one that went was John. Mum was a Jewish mother – the boy was everything. I don't feel bitter and twisted; neither does Liz. It's just the way it was.' Sue left Burnside High in the sixth form and went to Australia, then on to England. When she returned she enrolled at Canterbury University, but having left school early, she had to do a qualifying year before she could start a BA degree. 'At the end of that year I got a job and never went back, to my great regret.'

'The others go on about me being the favoured one,' counters John, 'but if there was anything to be shared out at home, Mum used to insist on equal portions. Serving dessert, it had to be the same for everyone.' For herself, she would be happy with whipped cream – as would he, even now.

> I love cream, she loved cream – it's an Austrian thing. I remember one time we went to the movies together in town on the bus. Coming home, we were walking from the bus stop in Clyde Road and she said, 'What do you want for dessert, toots?' – she always called me that [it rhymes with 'puts'] – and I said, 'Cream.' 'So do I,' she said. So I bought this half-pint of cream and she whipped it and that's what we had.

Ruth bequeathed her son a Continental taste in other meals too. Given a choice of hotel breakfasts, the Prime Minister is liable to go for the bread with ham or salami and cheese.

As he grew older, her influence on him was returned. The aspiring businessman was already following the share market in his teens and he encouraged his mother to dabble a little with her savings. He helped her manage her finances and apply for a mortgage, enabling her to give up the state house and buy a unit in Highsted Road, Bishopdale, the first home she had owned. Along the way he also convinced her to learn to drive. Sue remembers coming home from Australia on a visit in the winter of 1976 when John (15) had just got a driver's licence and his mother had bought a little Hillman Imp with the motor in the back. Sue and John set off to go skiing at Mt Hutt. Sue was driving when, halfway across the Rakaia bridge, the car skidded on ice and slammed into the side barrier.

> The car was a write-off but we managed to limp home. I made John drive and I cried all the way back, terrified at what Mum would say. When I walked inside she said, 'Are you all right?' I said, 'Yes, but I've smashed the car.' She said, 'Is John all right?' I said, 'Yes, but I've smashed the car.' Mum then said, 'Who drove home?' When I told her John did, she said, 'You get back in that car right now.' I had to get back in and drive because she knew I would lose my confidence. That was typical of Mum. She had spent a lifetime not being able to drive and she was determined that would not happen to me. She was great like that.

Ruth could be astonishingly blunt, though, with friends and neighbours – a common characteristic of Austrian women of her age, Liz was to discover when she went there. 'Mum said exactly what she thought – she didn't mince words.' The Keys' boarder Roger Norton came to know this side of her well. Norton had a steady girlfriend, Lois, and went overseas himself at the end of 1971 to give the relationship 'a bit of a test'. When he returned in 1973 and boarded with Ruth again, he and Lois had survived this test and were making preparations to get married in September.

'You two won't last,' Ruth told them, more than once. Lois used to get a bit indignant, says Norton. 'I would just reply, "We'll see about that."' The Nortons kept in frequent contact with her long after they were married, having her around for meals on occasion. Roger remembers Ruth sitting at their dinner table years after the wedding and reaffirming her prediction: 'You two won't stick it.' He enjoyed her manner and Lois says she learned to handle it. They have passed their fortieth anniversary.

The Nortons also had an experience of the Keys' quiet family solidarity. When Roger and Lois invited Ruth to their wedding she declined because they had not been able to make room on their guest list for her children. Roger admits he was 'a bit disappointed with that but she wasn't sore about it and we never mentioned it again'. Ruth's need to include her children possibly reflected the fact that the family had no relatives in New Zealand and almost none anywhere else. Sue felt that the absence of a wider family disconnected her from her own country somehow. 'The thing with John and me, [is that] even though we were born in New Zealand we were not Kiwi kids because everybody else had all these "rellies". We never had that. We had each other but we never had the whole extended family thing.' At Christmas time, when other families were getting together, Ruth used to take her children on a holiday by bus in the South Island, somewhere different every year.

While Sue includes John in her sense of alienation, nothing he has said suggests he felt the same. When Sue went on her OE – the overseas experience young New Zealanders seek as soon as they can – it was to search for an identity.

> I went to Vienna – I visited concentration camps and things like that. I had this huge need to know where I belonged. I obviously didn't belong in New Zealand. Though I was born here, neither of my parents were.

I didn't feel [like] a New Zealander, I do now, but in
those days I didn't.

Their one known relative in the world at that time was
Lottie, who came from London for Liz's wedding to Roger
Cave in Christchurch in 1974. 'She was the most outrageous
woman, she was fantastic,' says Sue.

> With blonde hair and blue eyes, she was gorgeous. As
> a milliner she had done hats for some famous people.
> When I went to England she would take me to amazing
> fashion shows with Yves St Laurent and all these
> people. It was the 1970s and the models were wearing
> nothing underneath. *Star Wars* came out and she took
> me to see it, in her seventies.

———

John, Sue, Liz and their families continued to get together
at Christmas for many years, even when John's financial
career had taken him overseas. He never missed a
Christmas, and seldom missed a daily call to his mother
wherever in the world he was. When the Nortons had her
around for a meal, Roger describes how she would update
them on John's progress.

> She used to tell us he was doing well at school, then
> well at varsity, and then over the years after he went to
> work she would talk about him being in a 'high flier'
> company. She'd say, 'He's earning big money, Roger,'
> and I'd think to myself, 'Oh yeah.' She'd tell us he was
> going up in the world, to Singapore, then London, and
> [then] I started to get the picture.

Ruth saw her son achieve the first goal of his life. He had made far more than a million dollars when she died aged 77 in 2000 – two years before he entered Parliament. For Liz, it is 'the saddest thing that Mum, who had such a hard life, did not live to see John become Prime Minister'. Near the end, Ruth wanted a Jewish funeral but was adamant she didn't want to be buried; she wanted to be cremated. 'The two don't go together,' Sue explains, 'but she talked the rabbi into it. She had a full Jewish funeral – black flag, the whole nine yards – and at the end was cremated. Only Mum could do that. We did laugh – only Mum . . .'

By then, Sue had adopted her mother's family name. When Sue's first marriage had ended and her ex-husband did not want her to keep his name, she had no wish to revert to Key. 'I had no fond memories of Dad and could see no reason to take his name. Plus, I always believed John was going to do something in public life, so I took Mum's maiden name. She was ecstatic, so proud.' Sue remarried after her mother had died but she decided to remain Sue Lazar, the only Lazar of her line, as far as she knows, left alive.

John Key at age four. FAMILY COLLECTION

TOP: George Key in London before meeting Ruth. FAMILY COLLECTION

BOTTOM: Ruth Key (rear) with her children (from left) Liz, Sue and John around 1969, the year their father died. FAMILY COLLECTION

John, aged 12, at his sister Liz's wedding at Riccarton House, Christchurch, 1974.

John and Bronagh Key after their wedding at Elizabeth House, Christchurch, on 1 December 1984. FAMILY COLLECTION

CHAPTER FOUR

Growing Up

Burnside High was New Zealand's largest school when a shortish, round-faced boy with a shock of fair hair was one of hundreds of new arrivals in 1975, self-conscious in their new grey pullovers with a wide green stripe at the neck and their green blazer with a cabbage tree on its pocket. The roll was so big the school had been divided into four divisions, each like a school in its own right. John Key went into the 'West' division where he was placed at first in a class below his ability. 'They told you they didn't do streaming but they kinda did.'

Because he was not taking a foreign language he was in a class that he topped too easily. He knew there was a higher level and he wanted to be there.

> Some of my mates were in the languages stream doing German. Mum knew German. I said to her one night, 'I should do German – you should have taught me German.' She was horrified. She said, 'You're never

going to Europe, what use is German? The whole
purpose of education is to do something with your life
and German will never do anything for you.'

Ruth's pragmatic attitude to education was to rub off
strongly on her son, influencing his choice of subjects not
just through high school but later at university.

Despite not taking a language, Key was soon promoted
to a 'professional' class. When he entered it, someone said
to him, 'Welcome to the big boys' club. Get used to coming
last.' Key might have smiled but inside he was saying, 'We'll
see.' His results were to put him about eighth or tenth out
of 30, 'but I wasn't anywhere near last – stuff that for a joke'.
Even 40 years later, his voice hardens and his eyes flash at
the memory, offering a glimpse of something well buried
beneath the affable, casual manner New Zealand knows so
well – something more than mere competitive spirit. The
confident boy from a poor neighbourhood possibly had
more than the usual need to prove himself.

Burnside High did not carry much social cachet in a city
where the school you attended is usually the first question
someone is asked, but it was not poorly regarded either.
It had been open only 15 years when Key was enrolled
and still looked new – a collection of multi-level class-
room blocks standing in open grounds and surrounded
by the young, middle-income suburbs of the city's northwest. It was rated very highly by teachers. Robin Duff,
twice national president of the Post Primary Teachers'
Association, joined the staff the year Key started, having
applied straight from teachers' college.

One of the reasons I was attracted to Burnside was that
it was developing a name as an open and lively school.

It very much endorsed difference and diversity. It was
one of the first schools to do away with the cane. I think
the only other one in Christchurch that had done so
was Linwood. Only six to eight schools in the country
were like that at the time. They gave up caning to get
guidance counsellor networks.

Duff taught English and knows he taught Key's class but,
like other teachers, cannot recall him. The boy who had
already made known to his family his ambition to make a
million dollars and become Prime Minister was neither a
standout nor a problem pupil, just one of thousands of faces
his teachers saw in their classrooms over the years. English
was probably not Key's strength in any case. His diction,
he admits, is 'terrible' to this day. He had not come from a
home that had many books.

English at Burnside was being integrated with social
studies, and the literature Duff put in front of Key included
New Zealand writers as well as Shakespeare and Victorian
novels. Key does not recollect much of it, though he
remembers Duff, and in a speech to school principals in
Auckland once cited him as an 'inspirational' teacher. Duff
was in the audience as president of the PPTA and claims
to have been embarrassed, but the tribute was probably
deserved. (Duff was an impressive speaker at Canterbury
University when the writer of this book was a contemporary
there.)

Public speaking turned out to be Key's forte at high
school, despite his diction. He enjoyed the combative
element of debating, preferring the role of third speaker
who has to demolish the arguments of the other team. He
still relishes the combat. 'I like Question Time in the House
when everyone thinks I'm going to get beaten up and I go,

"Oh well, I'll go and make a mess of them.'" He was in the school debating club from his second year and went on to win the Freeman Cup for debating and the public speaking prize in his final year. His sister Sue credits the prize to their mother's dinner-table debates. Although Key found public speaking came naturally, he does not think he does prepared speeches very well, even now. 'I do off the cuff much better. I prefer it when I can get up and say, here are three points and this is what we need to do.'

However, in the fifth form Key came home from school one afternoon and alarmed his mother with the news that he was thinking of leaving. He had started to follow horse racing, and a schoolmate, Rob, had a cousin who trained harness racers at Motukarara on Banks Peninsula.

> One day Rob came to me and said, 'We should get this job with my cousin and make some money. We can work with the horses and get all this inside information and pick the winners.' So we took the job cleaning out the stables and sometimes, if we were lucky, we got to drive the pacers. They go really fast. One day Rob told me he was going to leave school to become an apprentice trainer, and he did actually. I had done some work for [trainer and driver] Cecil Devine, who had a good horse on a neighbouring property, so I went home and said to Mum, 'Rob's leaving to be an apprentice trainer and I'm thinking about doing the same.' Mum just said, 'No.' I opened my mouth to argue and she said, 'That is the end of the discussion.' That was it.

Key admits it was not so much the horse work that appealed. 'I liked the idea of making money.' His mother was more amenable to him doing that.

I convinced Mum to let me set up a telephone account with the TAB. We were training this horse called Nugent Royale and it was quite a brilliant pacer in its day – well, we thought it was. It was doing good times. It went off to the races at Forbury Park [Dunedin] and it got bowled over. We had backed it a little bit, nothing too serious, but it was going to race somewhere else two weeks later. Rob and I knew how well it was doing, thrashing anything it was up against, so we backed it big time, like, $150. I was getting $2.54 a week as a paper boy at the time. So we really hit this thing and in the race it was miles out in front the whole way, then 200 metres from home it got a heart murmur and staggered over the line third. Pretty much all our money had been on for a win. It never raced again and I didn't go to the races again for about six months.

Mathematics was another strength at school, but when asked his favourite subject Key nominates economics. Rob Hughes, now head of commerce at Burnside, is one teacher who can clearly remember him. 'He certainly had an interest in economics and had his say in class, but I never thought, "Gee, there is a future Prime Minister." John is not super bright – not scholarship material. He was a good, steady guy, not one of the stars. He wasn't Robin Clements.' Hughes' star pupil, a year ahead of Key at Burnside, became an economist with the Reserve Bank and later chief economist for UBS in New Zealand. 'If I had to pick someone in my class who would be Prime Minister it would have been Robin Clements.'

Undeterred, John Key went through high school with his declared aims – to make a million dollars and become Prime Minister – undiminished. The politician he had most 'kinda admired', Muldoon, had been Prime Minister for most of those years and his methods were a subject of particular interest in an economics class. It was a period of rising worldwide inflation in the wake of oil price hikes by the OPEC cartel. Muldoon's first response to New Zealand's double-digit inflation and rising unemployment was to reduce spending and cut his budget deficit. Then, after the second oil shock in 1979, he reversed course, increasing the deficit to stimulate activity. It was a time of strikes, dawn raids on Polynesian overstayers, abortion law reform, extensions of shopping hours, United States warship visits, subsidies for farmers, and tax incentives for manufactured exports. According to Hughes, Key was not a defender of Muldoon in class. 'If he had been, he would have argued with me. Being an economics graduate of Canterbury [University], I was always keen on the free-market approach. I was very anti-Muldoon and he never argued with me.'

———

Key was in his last year of school, tutoring a fellow pupil at her home, when a friend of her younger sister called around. Bronagh Dougan was in the fifth form at Burnside. Her husband calls her shy, but that is only in comparison to him. Bronagh is short and quiet with warm eyes and a softly spoken but lively sense of humour. In those days, sport occupied much of her time outside school hours, as it did John's. She played softball and soccer; he played squash, and, as with most things he takes on, was very serious about it. They really did not see each other again until one evening when John came into the Russley Hotel restaurant where Bronagh was waitressing in her 'uniform of blouse and bow'. They made their first date, to go to the Industries Fair. 'We nearly didn't make it,' Bronagh reminds him. 'We first went to that Slazenger squash tournament and you drank all those whiskies which I thought was pretty revolting.'

Like John, Bronagh was the child of immigrants from Britain. Her parents had come from Northern Ireland in 1959 and both worked in Christchurch factories – her father at Feltex carpets, her mother at O'Brien's shoes. Her mother arranged a job for Bronagh in the school holidays, screwing studs into the soles of football boots. When the tax form needed a description of her job she wrote in 'stud screwer'. The office upstairs sent the form back, requesting her to please put something else. But the following year, when John got a holiday job there, she sent his form up as 'stud screwer' too.

John, meanwhile, found time away from squash to come and watch her play soccer. Bronagh recalls how she 'nearly got kicked off the pitch one day because he started chanting, "Off... off..."'

'She kicked a goalie in the head!' says John.

'She put her head between me and the ball,' she corrects him.

They both continued to live with their respective parents when John went to Canterbury University in 1980 and Bronagh followed two years later. He had warned her early that he intended to go into politics one day, but first he wanted to make that million.

Some students go to university to broaden their mind, liberate their thinking, rebel against the conventions around them, find themselves. Others go for a useful, lucrative qualification, the proverbial meal ticket. John Key was one of the latter. If there was any prospect that his education might have taken a more cerebral turn, it ended after his first year at university when he gave up his favourite subject, economics, and set himself to major in accounting.

It is a surprising decision for someone with a political career in mind. Economics would have been a particularly topical subject at Canterbury in the early 1980s. The faculty was, as schoolteacher Rob Hughes has said, a free-market school, though it also boasted the noted left-wing economist Wolfgang Rosenberg. When this writer was there, 10 years before Key, lectures by the likes of Ewen McCann on floating exchange rates that could, in theory, balance a country's external trade sounded quaintly academic. We were still in the post-war Keynesian consensus. The history we studied presented free markets as a wild, savage, primitive form of capitalism preceding the twentieth century's socially ordered enlightenment. Even businessmen at that time, all men, running their companies comfortably on a share of a protected market, were opposed to competition. They called it 'cut-throat'.

But by the time Key was studying economics, the election of Margaret Thatcher in Britain in 1979 had brought a new theory of economic management into practice. Free markets with floating currencies were elements of 'monetarism', which held that governments should concentrate on containing inflation, which could most effectively be done by limiting the amount of money and credit created by their banking system. Soon it was found easier and just as effective to control the cost of money (interest rates) rather than its quantity. Monetarism was invigorating economic debate.

Key's grades in first-year economics had been good enough for him to be one of a select group of students who received a letter from one of their lecturers, Frank Tay, urging them to take the subject further. Key's reply is one that Tay, in retirement, still vividly remembers. 'He told me he was going to major in accounting because he had studied company reports and found most of the directors were accountants. I was kind of disappointed.' Again, the decisive voice seems to have been his mother's. Ruth's practical priorities and high expectations still had a profound influence on the 19-year-old. 'I wanted to do economics; Mum stopped me. I could have said no, but in the end I accepted what she said. Directors all had accountancy degrees.'

His second year at university was the year of 'the tour'. The 1981 Springbok tour of New Zealand was by no means the first by an exclusively white South African rugby team in the apartheid era, but it would be the last. It did more than deeply divide public opinion on the question of whether a government should allow the tour to proceed; it went ahead against a scale of protest and police riot-control that New Zealanders never expected to see, shaking the country to its core. Yet Key cannot remember what side he took at the time.

When you watch him try to remember, it is clear he wishes he could. It would be easy for him to contrive a respectable, middle-ground position of opposition to both the tour and the right of a government to stop it. But honestly, he says, he cannot remember. Difficult as this is to credit, it is probably a myth of our own making that the tour polarised opinion so deeply that nobody was indifferent. In fact, of course, every issue leaves a large number indifferent. Politics for someone such as John Key bears no relation to the interests of someone such as the previous Prime Minister Helen

Clark. The distant, impersonal 'post-materialist' politics of nuclear disarmament, foreign wars, apartheid and the like were formative issues for her, not for him. They did not affect him personally or anyone he knew.

Key turned 20 while the Springboks were here. He was still living at home with Ruth, in her own unit by then. Bronagh was in her final year of school and she and John had just started going out. He had a car; life was good, with parties every weekend. By the second year of university, you knew how to pass. Some lectures could be skipped; end-of-year exams could be nailed with intensive 'cramming' from about eight weeks out. Key took no part in university politics or any political party. He spent much of his university years on a squash court.

He had taken up squash at school having pulled out of rugby around the age of 14 ('I didn't like being tackled'), and learned the sport with the same determination he applied to anything that mattered to him. He was not a natural with a bat or a racquet, as Roger Norton had observed at table tennis in Ruth's kitchen years before. A fellow player at the Burnside squash club, Chris Walsley, noticed that he 'wasn't naturally gifted but was very dedicated and focused, and very likeable'. Walsley remembers Key constantly asking questions of good players. 'He'd watch people and ask, "How did you do that?", "What training do you do?" – lots of questions.' Training five days a week from 6 a.m., Key made a Canterbury Colts team.

Key recalls that his game improved when he got contact lenses. He had been sitting in the back row of lectures in his first year at university when he realised he couldn't read the board. He wore glasses or contacts from that time until he had laser treatment sometime before going into politics. Another fellow squash player was Robin Clements, the future economist who tutored Key in economics that first year, and there were others Walsley remembers who, like Key, went on to work in finance.

> We were a group of guys who really enjoyed squash and the camaraderie of it. We used to go away on a lot of weekends playing tournaments around the South Island, particularly through the winter. John was a great team member because he was always so upbeat. I don't recall him ever getting angry on the court or swearing and carrying on. He was with Bronagh then and he wasn't a big drinker or anything. He trained hard because he really wanted to improve.

Long before he had completed his three-year accountancy degree, Key knew he had no wish to be a chartered accountant. But he was there to get a job and when accountancy firms had an open day at the university in his final year he went along. 'It was the conservative part of me thinking, "I've got to go and do this", and a couple of them offered me a job.' One of them was McCulloch Menzies, later Deloittes. Warren Bell, a partner in the firm, told him he could start as soon as he finished the university year or, as most graduates did, have a holiday until March. Key said he would be there on 10 November, the day after his last exam.

It was a strange time in the New Zealand business world. Muldoon, re-elected for a third term on a backlash from the Springbok tour, was at his wits' end to contain inflation. In June that year, 1982, he had imposed a freeze on all wages and prices. By November the freeze was proving popular. The public generally appreciated some relief from constant price rises. But neither Muldoon nor anyone else had any idea how to restore normal pricing without releasing all the pent-up increases. Originally to last a year, the freeze was extended in 1983 and still in force when Muldoon called a snap election in June 1984.

Meanwhile, John Key had not lasted long in accountancy. Among the firm's customers was an assembler of Space Invaders machines. He had been working with one of the partners on its books, essentially auditing them, which never makes accountants feel very welcome, and when they finished and went back to their office, they had a drink.

The way Key tells it, the 21-year-old said to the partner, 'Do you like your job?'

The older man said, 'Do you want the truth?'

'Yes,' said Key.

'I hate it,' the partner replied. He did it, he explained, to pay the bills for his hobby farm and race horses.

'This job is really boring,' Key told Bronagh that evening. 'Even my boss thinks it's boring. I'm leaving.'

He went to Lane Walker Rudkin where his sister Liz was a receptionist. He had been offered a job in their branded clothing division, Canterbury International. Canterbury was being run by one of the firm's bright young executives, Dave Phillipson, who was surrounding himself with other bright young tyros.

'You're projects manager,' he told Key.

'What does that mean?' Key asked.

'Just do stuff,' Phillipson replied.

Key was walking through the warehouse a short time later and saw thousands of items of men's coloured clothing that was practically unsaleable: red, blue, white and yellow trousers and the like. Designers had filled the stock room with the sort of eye-catching gear shops put in their windows. The colours draw men in but they do not buy it. When men buy pants they are navy, grey or khaki. The firm could not afford to be carrying so much excess stock and the new projects manager had to dump it, preferably far from any market Canterbury was developing. Key phoned around the world and made contact with a Londoner who reminded him of the character Arthur Daley on the television programme *Minder.* He told Phillipson he needed to go to London to see the man. 'It was the first serious overseas trip I'd ever had. I met the guy; he bought the lot and sold them to Poland and Russia.'

State-run economies of the Eastern Bloc were chronically short of consumer goods but New Zealand at that time was not exactly an open market either. Currency exchange was strictly controlled, both by the rate for the dollar and the quantity allowed, and goods could not be imported for sale except under licences issued by the government. While he was in London, Key saved his £30-a-day allowance for food, eating virtually nothing, so that he could bring back a microwave oven. It survives, 30 years on, in the Keys' beach house at Omaha.

As Key humped his microwave home on the plane, neither he nor anyone else suspected that New Zealand was about to undergo an economic revolution that would remove restrictions and tariffs on imports of the world's goods, services and capital. When Sir Robert Muldoon called the snap election in June 1984, he did not imagine the sequence of events he had unleashed. Nor could it have been seen by the Labour Party's finance spokesman, Roger Douglas, the main architect of the reforms that would ensue. They both caused the crisis that wrenched the economy onto a new course. Once the election campaign was under way, Muldoon accused Douglas of planning a devaluation of the dollar if Labour was elected. Douglas hardly bothered to deny it. With voters clearly ready for a change of government, the talk of devaluation started a run on the dollar. On the eve of the election, the Reserve Bank suspended all foreign currency trading.

The financial crisis became a public political drama on the Monday after the election when the Prime Minister-elect, David Lange, not yet sworn into office, made it known Muldoon was refusing to carry out the advice of the Reserve Bank, the Treasury and incoming government to devalue. Muldoon relented only when the party's deputy leader, Jim McLay, told him he would be removed by the National caucus if he did not follow constitutional convention and act on Lange's wish. The dollar was devalued by a massive 20 per cent and Douglas was in the driving seat for the reforms that followed.

Lange and Douglas 'opened the books', letting the press gallery see for the first time the Treasury advice Muldoon had long ignored. Journalists who read the books carefully could find the economic rationale for everything that followed. The country had been getting a low return on national investment with just about every sector protected, restricted, licensed and favoured, or not, by successive governments. The new government was going to neutralise all of its influence on commercial investment, exposing business decision-makers to unlimited competition and prices that would be set by competitive markets.

John Key followed these events from Christchurch and, as with the Springbok tour, it is hard to know what he thought at the time. Again, he had other things on his mind. In 1984 he and Bronagh were planning a wedding as soon as she finished university. They were married at Elizabeth House in Merivale on 1 December. But the financial deregulation gathering pace in Wellington was soon to mean a great deal to him – a personal fortune in fact.

CHAPTER FIVE

Currency Dealer

Newly married, John and Bronagh Key were in their Christchurch flat – the 'love nest', as they still refer to it – when a British documentary on television caught their eye. It was called 'A Day in the Life of a Foreign Exchange Dealer'. Key remembers it vividly. When it finished, he announced to Bronagh, 'I'm going to do that.'

It was 1985. To the surprise of many observers, not least National Party members in Parliament, when Roger Douglas floated the dollar it had not fallen through the floor. Quite the opposite: set free to find the value that currency traders would give it, the kiwi had flown. Opposition finance spokesman Bill Birch had nearly given up asking Douglas every day in the House what the dollar was trading at that day. He was no longer asking the question with the anticipation of disaster that was in his voice during the weeks immediately following the float. It was an understandable fear. New Zealand had, and still has, a chronic external deficit. The gap between its overseas earnings and payments meant the dollar should have fallen. But 'Economics 101' was not the whole story. Currency dealers and speculators were not much concerned about a country's external debt since that was now a matter for the private sector to manage. Currency markets were much more interested in the quality of a country's government as evidenced by its efforts to reduce inflation, budget deficits and public debt. On that score, the kiwi was starting to soar. As it approached the levels of the Australian dollar in 1985, foreign exchange dealers were said to be planning 'parity parties'.

'Forex' dealers were the new glamour boys of the business world. Typically young, smart, sharply dressed and dripping self-confidence, they were the shock troops of the new economy. Their instant collective response to political events, economic indicators and central bank pronouncements was a powerful running verdict on the quality of government everywhere. They did not make individual analytical judgements; they all moved on an instinctive sense of their collective response. 'Reef fish', David Lange dubbed them. They could make millions for their bank, sometimes hundreds of millions, on fractional movements of a currency, and they could lose it just as quickly. Watching the documentary, John Key, at 23, was thinking, 'That's gotta be the most exciting job you can do, isn't it?', and said out loud, 'I reckon I can do that.'

'Yes,' agreed Bronagh, 'probably.' She had been looking forward to their OE. She had been overseas only once, before they were married, when they went to Singapore on a package holiday. But the OE would have to wait.

John started writing to banks and got an interview with the Development Finance Corporation in Wellington.

> I went up there and they had quite a flash dealing room. The interview went well and at the end of the day they said, 'We're going to offer you a job.' 'Fantastic,' I said. Then they said, 'We don't want you to be a trader, we want you to be a salesman.'

Salesmen talk to clients and find out their currency exchange needs; traders watch the market and quote a rate for each exchange. Key was adamant, he did not want to be a salesman, he was going to be a trader. The woman at DFC was equally adamant and offered him $55,000 – nearly double the salary he was getting at Lane Walker Rudkin. He turned it down.

Then, Lane's put him in touch with an Australian stockbroking firm they had dealings with and the Keys went to Melbourne. It was only Australia, but for Bronagh it felt like her OE was finally about to start. After a couple of weeks, John got an interview with Elders Merchant Finance in Sydney. When he sat down with them it turned out they needed someone for their dealing room in Wellington but it was the DFC experience all over again. This time the interviewer who did not see a currency trader in John Key was a visiting bigwig from Wall Street, George Ziller.

> A real typical Wall Street banker. Red hair, beautifully groomed. I only went in to see him as a courtesy; everybody else had signed off on me. So I sat down with Ziller and all was going well, no issues, breezing our way through, and at the end he looked across the table and said, 'Well, John, you are one of the most impressive young men I have met and you are going to be great, but you will never make it as a trader and we won't be hiring you as one.'

This time, Key had support from those who had already offered him the job with the standard package of that time, $60,000 and a car. They haggled with Ziller and finally he relented but would agree to only $30,000 and no car. Key took it and told Bronagh he had the job he wanted at last. But there was a catch, he had to tell her. So much for the OE, they were going to Wellington.

────────

Elders Merchant Finance mainly served its parent company, Elders IXL. The company treasurer called the Wellington office one day when Key had not been there very long and wanted to sell about $A100 million at a rate slightly above where the market was. He asked Key what the market was about to do and Key said it was going to go up. He took Key's price and the new recruit started to trade with the sum he had bought. By the end of the day he had made well over $1 million, about a third of the earnings expected from the Wellington branch over the course of a year. When his boss asked how he had gone that day, Key said, 'I reckon you owe me that car.' Next morning, when Key was not in the dealing room as usual by 7 a.m., he took a call from his office on his 'brick' cellphone and told his boss he was at Archibald Motors with his eye on a brand-new Honda Civic. He got it and he wanted George Ziller to know.

The trick in currency trading is to guess whether the client on the phone asking you for a price wants to buy or sell the currency. They never tell you, although if it is a regular client and the sales team has been doing its job, the dealer will have a fairly good idea. Whether he does or not, he will quote two prices, a lower one to buy and a higher one to sell, each pitched to give the dealer a margin to make money if the market is moving in the direction he thinks. The margin will be in tiny percentages of a decimal point, but as a percentage of the sums traded the potential profits – or losses – are immense.

Elders' Sydney office used to send more-senior traders over to Wellington. One of them confessed to Key one day that he had lost several million in sterling and was hiding the trades from their superiors. 'You gotta tell them,' said Key. When the guy did he was fired.

> The next week an interest-rate trader came over. He turned up at 7 a.m. on a Monday and Macquarie Bank rang up for a price. I gave them a price a bit high and he said, 'What made you do that?' I said, 'Cos he's a buyer.' Half an hour later someone rang [for a price] and I said, 'Pitch it down.' He said, 'Why are you doing that?' I said, 'Cos he's a seller, trust me.' After two or three days the guy brought pizza over to our house and sat on the floor and said, 'I don't know anything about currencies, I don't like it, I don't want to do this, I'm going back to Australia and will ask them to send someone else.' So they did, but after a while they just stopped sending people.

They left Key to lead the small team. In 1987, a TVNZ *Close Up* programme in Wellington did an item on a day in the life of a foreign exchange dealer, featuring a fresh-faced John Key with wavy hair and wearing the collegiate, horn-rimmed glasses of the time. Sitting in front of small screens carrying lines of moving numbers, a telephone constantly at his ear, he was clearly the price-maker for the kiwi dollar in Elders' forex room. The 25-year-old, perhaps in conscious preparation for the political career he aspired to one day, let the television crew follow him to his Hataitai home, meet Bronagh and even film him in bed as he enacted the kinds of calls he took at any hour of the night from foreign traders wanting a price for the dollar. 'Most dealers are happy if they lose money on only one day out of five,' said the reporter. 'John Key has lost money on only one day this year.' In fact, Key insists now, they did not close on any day with a loss.

Those years, 1986 and 1987, brought New Zealand's first flush of free-market exuberance, culminating in a daring challenge for the America's Cup at Fremantle. The 'plastic fantastic' *KZ7* seemed to epitomise the idea that New Zealand was now competitive in the commercial world and anything was possible. The dollar during those first years of the float was highly 'volatile', in marketspeak. 'These days they trade on a one-point spread,' says Key. 'We would sometimes trade on 100-point spreads.'

He was not just a numbers man – the recruiters who had found him too personable for a dealer and better suited to building client relationships were not entirely wrong.

> I would spend more time talking to our big clients than the sales desk did. Goodman's and the Dairy Board and all these guys used to ring me. Julian Robertson, Paul Tudor Jones, Herman Rockefeller, Brierley's . . . Brierley's actually offered me a job – [former head of Brierley Investments] Paul Collins can't remember it, but it's true.

There was, and still is, a belief in the banking industry that the constant risks and adrenalin rush of forex dealing means it is strictly a young man's game, and that even the best are burned out by about the age of 26 or 27. Key never believed it. By the time he was 26 he was looking for bigger deals than he could do at Elders. 'What I realised after a while was that conglomerates shouldn't own banks. Their banks haven't got the capital and the structure they need.' Some of those big clients who called him for advice were looking to place bigger orders, with bigger risks, than the Wellington branch of Elders Merchant Finance could take. The bigger the orders a dealer can handle, the better his understanding of what is happening in the market at the time. Key's reputation in NZ dollar trading by 1987 was such that almost every week he was getting another job offer. In 1988 he accepted one.

It came from Auckland where the big American finance company Bankers Trust was making a belated entry into the small but lively New Zealand market. Gavin Walker, now chairman of ASB Bank, the Commonwealth Bank of Australia and the New Zealand Superannuation Fund, was chief executive of Bankers Trust NZ.

> We were trying to build a foreign exchange dealing capability and so we looked around at the talent available in the New Zealand market at that time and one name that constantly came up was John's. That surprised me because he was not working for one of the established players. He seemed to have a disproportionate profile relative to the size of investment banking and trading that Elders was doing. Most large international institutions who had exposure to the NZ dollar or were trading in the dollar would speak to John and if they couldn't take the credit risk in Elders' name they would do the business elsewhere. That was one of the reasons John came.

Just before he left Wellington, though, on his last day there, 31 August 1988, Key and his successor as Elders' local head of foreign exchange, Paul Richards, went for a farewell lunch at Plimmer House restaurant that would raise some questions for him in his political career. It was a long lunch – the bill would run to $342.40. They had just finished the entrée when Richards took a call to return to his office to see an Elders executive from Australia, Ken Jarrett. He was away for 45 minutes. Richards was later given immunity when he gave evidence in a Melbourne court about a phony foreign exchange transaction, one of two that led to prison sentences for Jarrett and New Zealander Allan Hawkins, head of the investment company Equiticorp which collapsed the following year.

Investigators of the sham transactions, covering an illegal payment called the 'H-fee', interviewed Key to corroborate Richards' testimony that he had been called away to meet Jarrett that day. Twenty years later, when the Labour Party raised the subject on the eve of the 2008 election, Key said his advice was never sought on the transactions, that he had had no knowledge of them and took no part in them. The *New Zealand Herald* sent an investigative reporter, Eugene Bingham, to check the 13,000 pages of the case file in the Melbourne Office of Public Prosecutions. Bingham found no evidence Key had been involved. Key had been on 'gardening leave' since June when he accepted the job with Bankers Trust, but he has noted that had he stayed at Elders it would have been him meeting Ken Jarrett that day.

John and Bronagh moved to Auckland. On his first day at Bankers Trust, Gavin Walker gave him 'names' representing hedge funds, international investment banks, commercial banks, sovereign funds, speculators in the NZ dollar and currency speculators at large. One of them was an options trader at Bankers Trust in New York, Andy Krieger. The previous year Krieger had been convinced the kiwi was grossly overvalued and had sold it down so heavily that somebody in the New Zealand government – Key thinks it was David Lange – phoned Bankers Trust New York to demand they stop attacking the currency. Key will never forget the first call he took from Krieger. 'His first question to me was, "What's the GDP of New Zealand?"'

Key himself may have started a run on the dollar the day Roger Douglas was dismissed as finance minister, though he doubts he did. He and Bronagh had been at a funeral that morning for an infant nephew who had drowned in a swimming pool. After the service, Key turned on his car radio and heard the news from Parliament that Douglas had called a press conference for 2 p.m. Anybody who had been following New Zealand politics that year could guess what was coming. It was also obvious by then that Douglas's departure would change nothing. The cabinet had supported him at every turn in Lange's solo attempt to stop further economic reform. David Caygill would be the new Minister of Finance and reforms would go on. All this, Key must have known.

Yet that morning, 14 December 1988, he did not go on to the child's wake; he went straight back to his dealing room. 'I expected there would be mayhem but in fact it was very quiet. I said to them, "Gee, you better sell."' He sat down and began shedding the kiwi. He has told the *Herald* he sold 'this massive amount'. The dollar tumbled as all traders covered their positions. Then, just before 2 p.m., Key began to buy back in at the low rate the dollar had reached. They were trading till nine o'clock that night.

> I knew I'd made a lot – it was millions. I remember Gavin coming over and asking, 'Is it half a million?' It was way more than that. I don't remember if it was one, two or three million. It was a record for what I'd made and certainly the firm did very, very well.

Key explains that day as a classic case of the trading adage, 'Buy the rumour, sell the fact'. It was also classic mob behaviour. Probably all New Zealand traders were fairly certain Douglas's exit would change nothing, but fairly certain is not enough in a foreign exchange market. 'Your view of [events] that day would be different,' says Gavin Walker, 'if you had $US500 million at risk.'

> Traders assume the worst. They are operating under limits as to how much loss they can sustain and they have to make quick judgements. So they close it down, listen to the press comment and see what happens. He [Key] would have been watching the kiwi fall and working out how much profit he was making at each point if he closed that position out by buying the dollar. His position was so large when he bought back in that he probably forced the kiwi up. He had to be very careful because if the market knew he was short and was trying to square his position, the market would have bid against him. He had to be very careful and selective about how he bought those dollars back. That is the art and skill in all of this.

Foreign exchange dealing is not a career choice many might find compatible with political ambition. Politicians of all stripes are driven by a sense of the national interest even if they disagree on how that interest is defined. When John Key became a dealer, he concedes, 'I wasn't thinking it would make me a better politician, I was just thinking, "This is what I want to do and I reckon I can be good at it."' But, as he also points out, currency trading and politics are not poles apart.

> Everything flows through currencies. They are like a barometer of world events. I remember being an expert on Scud missiles because that's what they were firing in the first Gulf War. Currencies are quite unpredictable, they should trade on orthodox responses, but often when [Reserve Bank governor Don] Brash cut interest rates the exchange rate went up. Interest rates and exchange rates don't follow in a linear way. I loved the speed and adrenalin of it and the fact that you were only as good as your last trade. You had to be on your game the whole time.

In his view, it is a market that does serve a national interest.

> There is obviously a highly speculative end of the markets, but there is another group that simply needs liquidity. Fonterra needs a currency market, banks borrowing overseas need one. Financial markets provide much greater efficiency for consumers around the world by facilitating international trade and borrowing. Of course, there is a speculative element to that, but if I make money as a currency trader does it mean you the client have to lose money? Is it a zero-

sum game? The answer is no, because you are more efficient in the price you have received and we can all make money.

Dealers who make money for the bank do very well for themselves. Although they are not paid on commission, they receive a salary and an annual bonus that reflects their performance. When John Key was manager of the Bankers Trust foreign exchange desk in the early 1990s, the salary and bonus packages typically ranged from $250,000 to $600,000 annually. Every year he would negotiate the rates for his team with Walker.

> Each time he made those recommendations to me he did so without the knowledge of what he was going to be paid. That would be the last discussion we would have. At no time did he promote himself and tell me how much I should pay him. That is not very common among finance traders.

It is a fair bet Key was at the top of that remuneration range. He was not just managing the dealing room – by 1995 he was also on the board of Bankers Trust NZ and poised to go much higher in the world.

CHAPTER SIX

London, New York

When Bronagh Key finally got her chance to experience living overseas it could hardly have come at a more inconvenient time. Her daughter Stephanie was just two years old and Bronagh was expecting their second child in two weeks. The family had been only nine months in a new house they had had built in Arney Crescent, Remuera. But it was a moment when it had become difficult for John to continue working at Bankers Trust in Auckland. By the end of 1994 he was being courted by BT offices in Singapore and New York. In New York they wanted him to be the dollar–deutschmark trader – 'which is like playing for Chelsea in the premiership'. But New York did not appeal as a place to live. 'In hindsight it was all completely wrong. We could have lived in Connecticut and commuted. But Singapore seemed like an easier place to be. Bronagh had always liked Singapore. It was halfway. New York just seemed a long way away.' They were close to their families in Christchurch and John's mother was now 72.

Safe, clean Singapore, though, was not so safe in the BT dealing room. The Singapore branch invited Key up for a week.

> It was theoretically a business trip but they got me to trade for the week. They were massive speculators – they used to take $US100 million positions. So I was doing this really big stuff, and there was little love lost there between the dealers. I was sitting there one day about three minutes to twelve when the market in Singapore closes for lunch and one of them said, 'Make me a price for $500 million.' I said, 'What are you gonna do?' He said, 'I'll tell you when you make me a price.' So I made him a price, then they started trading away from me. I realised I'm getting half-hammered here, so I got out of it.

Nevertheless, at the end of the week when BT Singapore offered him a job, he said yes.

> I felt it was time to move on. They told me they'd spoken to Australia and Gavin and everyone was good about it. But they told me not to speak to Gavin. I came back to Auckland and felt uncomfortable not saying anything to him. We were really good friends and I thought it odd he wasn't saying anything. I waited a few weeks and then Singapore admitted they hadn't told him. So I went in and told him.

Gavin Walker did his utmost to keep his top dealer, mapping out a career path that included Walker's own job. Ironically, when Walker had first interviewed Key back in

1988 and asked about his ambitions the 27-year-old had said, 'I want your job.' Now his horizons were wider. When the New Zealand and Australian branches heard he was leaving, however, there was a 'meltdown'. 'The feeling was it was a Singapore takeover,' he explains. 'That I would take everybody out of New Zealand and Australia and build a Singapore hub. It wasn't true, but that's what they thought.' The word came down from the Bankers Trust hierarchy that Key had to stay where he was, so he quit. There had always been plenty of other job offers, among them an offer from one of the big five Wall Street investment banks, Merrill Lynch.

The offer had come from Merrill's Hong Kong office. Key called and was asked, 'How soon can you get here?' It was a Wednesday. Key said he would be there by Friday. He went, they wanted him to run their Asian foreign exchange desk from Singapore, and on the following Monday he resigned from Bankers Trust. He marvels that Bronagh could make the shift two weeks before their son Max was due. In hindsight, they agree, she should have stayed behind and had the baby in New Zealand. For one thing, Singapore did not admit women who are more than 28 weeks pregnant. 'We had to sign all sorts of forms to say the child would not be Singaporean, though Max [18] now jokes that he should go back for his national service.'

At the time, there was hardly a moment to think. Key chose a house before Bronagh and Stephie came up and Merrill Lynch transferred all their household effects. 'They air-freighted all of it – sofas, the whole nine yards – put everything on a Singapore Airlines 747 and it arrived five days later.' Their furniture could not half-fill the big house that John had chosen in leafy Chancery Lane, not far from the city centre. It had a lot of marble in it, Bronagh recalls.

'Marble and maids,' adds John.

'It was a vast thing,' agrees Bronagh, 'we rattled around in it. We lived on the first and second floors and there were two more floors above that.'

If Key was impressed with his new firm's furniture-moving, he was not as impressed with its foreign exchange operation. He had been Merrill Lynch's head of foreign exchange for Asia for about three months when one of the bank's big traders in London, who wanted to make some changes, came to Singapore to talk to him. Key and the senior trader, Australian Steve Bellotti, went out to dinner and Bellotti asked Key what he thought of Merrill's set-up.

'You want me to be honest?' said Key. 'It sucks.' He added that he was thinking of going back to Auckland.

Bellotti countered with an offer for Key to come to London and run the firm's global foreign exchange. 'If you don't turn it around in 12 months I'll sack you,' he said.

'If I can't make it work in 11 months,' replied Key, 'I'll quit.'

So, after less than a year in Singapore, they were on the move again.

Key had never wanted to live in London. 'I thought it a dismal place.' But it had become a global financial centre to rival New York and John Key was to become an important figure in foreign exchange on both sides of the Atlantic. Merrill Lynch was in essence a massive stockbroking firm with about 15,000 rich private clients. Through a network of advisers, each with about 100 clients, the firm could find investors for any financial asset.

If you were IBM and you wanted to issue commercial paper or bonds or stock you virtually had to deal with Merrill Lynch. But in foreign exchange we used to go to other banks, almost like a customer. So in London I said, 'Look, we have all these customers doing all their trading with us in bonds and equities and everything else, but they are not doing foreign exchange with us. What we can do is build a liquidity distribution and go to these clients and say, "We're not asking you to do anything at extra cost to you, we're asking you to do your foreign exchange through us."'

He took his proposal to the other big Wall Street investment houses such as Morgan Stanley and Goldman Sachs. 'I went out to lunch with guys from Goldman's and said, "I'm going to go interbanking, you guys should come with me. The investment banks can go in there and beat them all." They said, "You're mad." I said, "You're mad – you're in the Dark Ages."' The big banks that dominated currency trading, such as Deutsche, Citibank and Chase, were equally dismissive of the idea.

They thought it was a joke when we started. I remember when Citibank rang up and said, 'Oh, little Merrill Lynch is going to make us a price?' I said, 'Yes, we can do that.' In the end business flowed into us because we had all these cross-collateral agreements. We were cross-selling several products off one bit of margin. We could go to big hedge funds and say, 'Give us a billion dollars and we'll let you buy bonds, stocks, equities, we'll revalue everything.' So they got massive leverage off small amounts of capital.

Soon Goldman's, Morgan Stanley and the rest followed Merrill's lead. With so much going on in New York it must have been tempting to move there. But Bronagh and the two children had quickly settled in London, in a house they liked in Barnes. Key became a frequent trans-Atlantic commuter. He would take the 6.40 flight out of Heathrow on a Monday night after a day's work in London, arriving in New York around 1.30 a.m. In his hotel he would take a sleeping tablet ('or you just couldn't do it'), then wake in time to do a day's work there on Tuesday. He would sometimes stay three days in New York and then repeat the overnight commute, taking a Thursday-night flight from JFK, landing at Heathrow at 6 a.m., showering and shaving and working Friday in London. In good weeks he could finish in New York in time to catch a Concorde flight on Thursday afternoon. It left at 1.30 p.m. and got in at 9 p.m. 'That was very nice. You got to sleep in your own bed.'

There were periods when he made the trip three times in 10 days; other times he wouldn't need to do it for three weeks or a month, but it averaged out that he was on Wall Street about every second week. No wonder his weekends were quieter than the excesses of the financial trading stereotype, though Key witnessed plenty of that.

> There were guys working for me . . . On Mondays they'd say, 'How was your weekend?' And I'd say, 'Oh great, we took the kids to a duck pond, Saturday night we went out for dinner, what did you do?' They'd go, 'I took the Brazilian lap dancer over to the US on Concorde and had a bit of fun.'

Bronagh recalls friends who would go to a resort in the middle of the Indian Ocean where they worked out they were spending $US1 a second while they were there – 'why would you?'

'It was just stupid,' agrees John. 'Guys that worked for me had jets and just blew their money. Lots of people around us were doing that. In the end they came away with no money and they had been earning around the same levels as me.'

Key will not divulge how much he did earn at Merrill Lynch but will give a good hint. When he came home, after six or seven years at the top of international currency trading, the *National Business Review* put him on its 'Rich List' with an estimated personal wealth of $50 million.

'They're just guessing,' he says.

Maybe, but when it is suggested to him that $50 million seems a little high for someone on a salary and bonuses for that time, he explains that not long before he joined Merrill Lynch in 1995 its remuneration packages had been typically cash, stock and stock options in a ratio of 40:40:20. By the time he arrived, the firm had been having financial problems and losing too many staff to higher offers from other banks, so it had introduced more flexible payment 'pots'. Employees could vary the ratios. The younger ones with large mortgages, or the lifestyle just described, wanted most of their pay in cash. Key was the opposite.

> When they came to me at the end of 1995 I said, 'I don't want cash, pay me 100 per cent in stock and options.' I was convinced the stock was undervalued. So they paid me a bit of cash but not much. The proportion of stock was much higher and in the years I was there it went up about seven times. You can do the maths. If it was a $2 million [annual] package it ended up being $11 million. So even if I paid $4 million in tax, I was doing all right.

By the time he left the firm at the end of 2001 he would have been paid in Merrill Lynch's appreciating stock for nearly seven years. That NBR estimate of $50 million was probably close to the mark. While Key is in politics it sits in a blind trust. His lawyer chose the trust managers. Key does not know them. He gave them a mandate to invest conservatively (lower risk and returns) and he is supposed to receive an updated figure for his capital every year. 'For the first three years they forgot and I didn't ask them.' They have given him an annual number every year since but do not tell him what is in the portfolio. 'I want to be able to look down the camera 100 per cent and say, "I don't have a clue what I own."' He is not particularly concerned. 'The value of our properties is tens of millions so even if the trust blew us up completely I'd still be okay.'

———————

John and Bronagh had left New Zealand intending to be away only a couple of years. They did not sell their newly built house in Remuera until it was clear they were going to be away much longer and, even then, they had their eye on a new property in Auckland. Ever since she had come to live in the city, Bronagh had loved Parnell. The old inner-city suburb with its quaint shops, art galleries, boutiques and fine restaurants was no longer the most fashionable real estate in Auckland. It had been eclipsed somewhat by the gentrification of equally old Freemans Bay, Ponsonby and Herne Bay on the western side of the central city. But to a newcomer to Auckland there was, and is, no contest. Parnell is more leafy and stately, and it is quieter now that galleries and fine dining can be found in many other parts of the city.

Driving around Parnell, Bronagh used to look longingly

at a spare section beside an old house in St Stephens Avenue. She often said when they passed, 'I'd like to live there.' They had been in London a couple of years when John made a quick trip home to visit his mother, and a friend in Auckland phoned to tell him that 'Bronagh's section' was for sale. He went there, saw that the house and section were on the market and phoned the agent.

> He came around and said it's on for, let's say, $2.7 million. I offered him $2.4. He said that was what it previously sold for and told me there was a guy willing to pay the asking price but hadn't yet fronted with the money. I said, 'Here's the deal: it's $2.4 million cash and you've got 15 minutes. I'm flying out shortly.' He started to play games. I said, 'It's 13 minutes, take it or leave it.' He said, 'Well, there's this other guy . . .' I said, 'There's always another guy, you've got 11 minutes.' [Listening to this yarn, Bronagh looks glad she wasn't there.] So anyway he took it. I signed the papers at the airport. Then, when the plane landed at Singapore, the agent was on the phone offering us more than we had paid to walk away from it. Turned out there *was* another guy, who hadn't believed we existed, and he was offering $100,000 more than we'd paid. Would we sell? I said, 'Nah.'

It is a story that Key could use to illustrate a theory of why some people get rich and the majority do not. Most people, he explains, take their profits too early and cut their losses too late. If they buy a house for $500,000 and a month later somebody offers them $600,000, it is human nature to take the money and dine out on their good fortune. Conversely, if they put that $500,000 house on the market and the best offer it brought was $350,000, they'd hold on to it. A good dealer would not. As soon as he realised the asset was losing value he would get what he could for it and put the money into a new, hopefully better, investment. Key explained this in a different context.

> We went to see *The Wolf of Wall Street* with Max and afterwards he was asking a million questions about trading strategies. I said to him, 'How many days do I need to make money to be successful as a currency trader?' He said, 'More days than you lose, basically.' I said, 'No, that's not right. You can make money two days out of 10 as long as you make more money on those days than you lose on the other days.' Not many do; every natural instinct in the human brain is to let your losses run and take your profits early.

At Merrill Lynch, Key used 'profitability profiles' for each of his traders showing the days they had made money and the days they had lost it. Some who made money most days never made enough to make up for their big losses on other days. 'They got out too soon on good days and never cut their losses quickly enough on the others.' Yet he did not agree with Merrill's policy to retrench on staff quickly when the weather turned rough. The world went through a succession of rough patches during his time there: a Russian debt crisis, the Asian financial crisis of 1997–98, the dot-com crash of the late 1990s. Each time he had to sack members of his team, earning him the title 'the smiling assassin'. He has said he could see no sense in firing people in areas such as foreign exchange and derivatives where money can be made in falling markets, and told the New York managers in 1999, 'You've got this wrong, not only will you be losing the thing that's making you money, you'll have to hire them again.'

He was a manager more than a trader in his years at Merrill Lynch, though there were days when he would sit down in the dealing room and quote prices, 'just to keep my hand in, show them how it's done'. To do it well, he needed complete confidence in his instincts. 'I used to be able to sit there and look at two digits and tell whether the price was going up or down.' As in any profession, there were changing ideas about what mattered. When he started, the most important statistic the market awaited was the 'M1' money supply figure from the United States, the measure of the quantity of cash in circulation. 'Every second Friday, the Americans would produce their number for M1 and we would all rush around with sell or buy orders. Then one day, it didn't matter anymore. Crazy.'

Those who worked alongside Key in trading rooms all remark on his calm, an unusual quality in an industry more commonly associated with what Gavin Walker calls 'very arrogant, self-willed, high-belief, very intense individuals'. Key, as Walker remembers him, was 'never arrogant, always complimented his team'.

> He really believed it was a team effort because no person on a foreign exchange desk can be the recipient of all the information about what is happening in a given market at a given moment. He had a great team of people around him, gave them confidence, argued for them in terms of promotion and bonuses, and never put his own interests ahead of theirs.

John Hunt, a derivatives trader (options and swaps) on Key's desk at Bankers Trust Auckland, remembers him as 'a very positive influence in the dealing room, remarkably easy to deal with'.

> Because the industry paid a lot of money it could attract people who were not people you would trust or invite back to your home. John always struck you as an extremely honourable person – you felt comfortable dealing with him. If he told you something was the case, it was, whereas with a lot of people you dealt with, you always took what they said with a grain of salt.

Key agrees that his ability to keep cool was unusual in the industry. 'It is full of what we affectionately call phone-throwers. They chuck their toys. It suited me.' Steve Bellotti told a Bloomberg interviewer in 2010 that Key had succeeded in currency trading without taking big risks. 'He was not the king of volatility. He was not the superstar outstanding athlete. He was consistent sometimes to the point of being boring. He was also a great team builder.'

At the dawn of 2001, the year he would turn 40, John Key decided it was time to think about starting on the second big ambition of his life. He had never wavered in his intention to enter politics. Back at Bankers Trust he had told them about writing to Rowling when he was young, and during his years in London, when Gavin Walker was over and they would catch up for lunch, his old boss gained the impression Key's desire to go into politics was getting steadily stronger.

Key went to New York early in 2001 to tell the head of the investment bank, G. Kelly Martin, he was leaving. Martin later told the *Herald* he thought his head of global foreign exchange and European derivatives was 'having a midlife crisis' and tried to talk him out of it. He offered him the position of global head of sales, in charge of the whole debt business side of Merrill Lynch. Key seriously considered it. If he took the post, which would mean moving to New York, he knew his political ambitions in New Zealand would be buried. 'I wouldn't have come back.'

By then he was on the boards of a number of Merrill Lynch subsidiaries in Europe, including the board of its Capital Markets Bank that had been set up in Ireland. He had transferred much of Merrill's London business to Dublin to take advantage of Ireland's low corporate tax rates. He was also doing an e-commerce project for the company in association with Harvard University. Currency trading margins were being squeezed by new information technology that let clients see the market as clearly as dealers could. Key believes the narrowing of margins contributed to the global financial crisis as dealing houses tried to maintain their profitability. They compensated for the reduced margins by increasing their volumes exponentially and relying on leveraged accounts like hedge funds with $1 billion on which they were trading $50 billion.

When he visited the firm in later years he was astonished at the risks it was carrying. Merrill Lynch was the third of the big five Wall Street investment banks that could not sustain its losses after the 2007 subprime mortgage collapse and in September 2008 it was bought by Bank of America. Trading as Merrill Lynch Wealth Management, it retains a network of 15,000 financial advisers and, with $2.2 trillion in client assets, it is said to be the world's largest brokerage. Had Key stayed at Merrill Lynch he would have been, Gavin Walker believes, 'without doubt a candidate to be their global chief executive – he was in that echelon just below'.

But in 2001 he had made up his mind to go. He agreed to stay only another year or so, which Martin wanted him to spend in Sydney straightening out the firm's debt market desk there. In Sydney he continued to work on the e-commerce project which required occasional trips to New York. He was due to fly there the day after 9/11. The leader of his e-commerce project, Harvard IT expert Michael Packer, was killed in the attack on the World Trade Center.

Sydney was just a stepping stone for John Key on his journey back to New Zealand. He had made about 50 times the million dollars of his childhood ambition. The Keys returned to build a $5 million mansion in St Stephens Avenue – 'the house that Merrill built', John would call it. They had a beach house at Omaha north of Auckland, they kept their London house, and they bought a Hawaiian holiday home for a reported $US3.2 million in the exclusive Wailea resort on Maui. More than 12 years after quitting the financial world with wealth estimated at $50 million, the Keys remain content. Says John:

> We are not ridiculously wealthy. There are a lot of people with more – the Graeme Harts of this world. There are a lot of people never seen on the Rich List who have lots of money. We are not in that category. We could have made more money, but it was a question of what that would have delivered us. Would it have been life-changing?

'I think it is fair to say we are conservative with money,'

Bronagh adds. 'We have a nice home and nice holidays. We don't want for things, but we're not silly either.' Sitting in that 'nice home', John agrees.

> Yes, we built a big house but this house is now worth substantially more than when we built it. It has been a good asset. We just don't have an expensive lifestyle really. We eat well and drink nice wine but don't feel the need to drink Châteauneuf-du-Pape. If we go to LA, we fly business class because it's a long flight.

'The kids fly economy,' interjects Bronagh.

'They want to,' says John.

'Well, we tell them they are flying economy,' Bronagh counters, 'and they are now at that age that it really is not cool to be in business class with your parents.'

Why, though, with the financial world at his feet, did John Key make the decision to come back?

> Well, three things. First: in our hearts we wanted to live in New Zealand. Stephie was eight, Max six. Max had never lived in New Zealand and Stephie had spent most of her life away. Secondly: I absolutely wanted to do it [politics]. I used to say to people, I didn't want to die wondering. I didn't want to sit back one day and think, 'I could've, might've, should've . . .' Third: We had enough money. Okay, we could have made tens of millions more, but we had enough.

CHAPTER SEVEN

Down and Dirty

John Key's first political speech was abysmal. He had been invited to address a National Party regional conference in Auckland, and in the words of one of those present, former Prime Minister Dame Jenny Shipley, it was 'terrible'. 'He was dry, boring, not animated, and I thought, "Oh my God . . ." The content was excellent, 10 out of 10, but it was too long and it rated 2 out of 10 for political nous.'

That was May 2001. Key had made known to National his interest in standing at the 2002 election and the party was keen to hear this high-flying Kiwi in the financial world who was in Sydney working out his last year with Merrill Lynch. Now that he was taking the leap from the pinnacle of one career to the starting point of another he was clearly going to need some political tuition and Key, as usual, was prepared to ask questions, watch, listen and learn, as Shipley recalls.

He had decided that if he was going to come into
politics it was to be Prime Minister and all he wanted
to know was, 'How do you do this really well? What do
I need to know? What do I need to do?' He just wanted
a crash course and I was one of a number of people I
know he spoke to.

Shipley had met him a couple of years earlier when she
was still in office. Key's sister Liz at Lane Walker Rudkin
in Christchurch had mentioned his political intentions to
National Party president John Slater, also in the textile
business and a frequent visitor at Lane's. 'Tell him to give
me a call,' said Slater.

When Key brought the family home for Christmas in
1998 he was invited to the Coromandel at New Year for
a brunch at Slater's Pauanui house. A number of National
ministers were there. It is not unusual for young risers in
corporate life to approach National Party officials with
a gleam in their eye. It is less common for them to be
put in front of the Prime Minister. Was the young man
from Merrill Lynch a dilettante? Having achieved all he
wanted in global finance, and made his fortune, was he
looking to politics just for some personal fame, a sense of
self-importance, a pleasant social life in the company of
like-minded fellows? Key passed Shipley's 'smell test' for
application and character. 'Yes, he was wealthy and probably
could have chosen any career, but I was satisfied in early
conversations, and these were not prudish conversations,
that he had the public interest in his mind.'

His credentials were exactly what the party needed at
that time. A large number of senior ministers, including
Bill Birch, were going to retire at the 1999 election and
National's ranks would be thin in financial experience. So

Shipley encouraged him, 'but not to the point of saying, we have to have you, won't you please come home. We never did that.' Key in any case was not ready to come across to politics just then. He had joined the party but the Shipley government was heading for defeat in 1999. He had his eye on 2002.

By the time Key was ready to stand for Parliament, Helen Clark was Prime Minister and proving to be an impressive one. The public saw a leader of sound judgement, conspicuous competence and even a sense of humour previously known only to close friends and colleagues. Labour was approaching 50 per cent support in the polls and National was floundering. Shipley had been replaced by Bill English, but having been finance minister in the final phase of her government, English was not the new face parties usually need if they are to recapture public attention.

Slater meanwhile had been toppled from the party presidency by Michelle Boag. Boag is a singular presence in New Zealand politics, a forceful party insider who does not adhere to the code that she can be heard but not seen or quoted. She made it public when she became National's president that she was on a mission to rejuvenate the party and purge its caucus of 'dead wood'.

When Key came home to launch a political career he had hoped to go into Parliament on National's list – the order of candidates to be awarded seats on the basis of the party's proportion of the total vote at the election. 'I'd been out of the country, I didn't know anyone. I just thought that would be the route.' Boag had other ideas. For one thing, it was going to be a 'tide out' election for National and not many on the list would get in unless they were also standing in a safe electorate. For another, Key was unknown. He might have been a name in currency trading but he had no public recognition in New Zealand. His name had never been in the paper, not even on the business pages.

'He was an unknown and had no history in the party,' Boag explained, 'so it would be difficult to justify.' He was not Don Brash. The Reserve Bank governor was well known and had been an extremely effective presenter of monetary policy before Boag encouraged him to move into Parliament in 2002. Brash was given a slot as high as number five on National's list. Key, by contrast, was given a baptism of fire.

Boag invited him to accompany her to a Rotary meeting at Kumeu where she was going to give a speech. 'It was to show him retail politics, because clearly he hadn't had any of that sort of experience. I said, "Come and have a look and see what happens."' Kumeu was in the Helensville electorate, a seat that a boundary revision had made even safer for National than it had been as Waitakere. Its MP, Brian Neeson, had made his name in West Auckland local government but since going to Parliament on the high tide for National in 1990 had done nothing to distinguish himself. He was at the Rotary meeting and not amused. He told Boag so. 'Brian had a go at me afterwards, saying, "Why did you bring this guy out to my electorate?" I said, "People who are interested in standing for Parliament have to see what happens on the hustings, what sort of audience you get and how you deal with it."'

Clearly she also wanted Key to see Neeson, size him up and realise he was beatable. He was not the only sitting National MP who would face a challenge that year. Out on Auckland's southern rural fringe Warren Kyd was about to be unseated for Clevedon by a formidable newcomer, Judith Collins. Kyd went quietly by comparison to Neeson. 'In hindsight,' says Key, 'I didn't realise how hard it would be.'

If a National MP has lost favour with the party leadership, he or she had better have enough friends and supporters enrolled as members of the party in their electorate to withstand a challenge. Candidates are selected by a panel of at least 60 delegates, one for every 15 members in the electorate. If there are 900 local members, they can fill the panel. If they cannot, the rest of the delegates are appointed by the party's regional office. If he had to mount a challenge for a seat, Key's preference was probably Tamaki. It was closer to his home, and its MP, Clem Simich, had never made a national impact. But Simich was impregnable, as Boag knew. 'John couldn't have beaten Clem; [All Black] David Kirk couldn't beat Clem.' Simich always had enough supporters in his seat to stack a selection panel. On that score, Neeson had not done too badly either. He had enrolled a sufficient number to have a clear majority of the 60 delegates. Reports at the time suggested he had 42. Boag says he had 38. 'He should have won, because the 38 were all his people.'

But once the delegates are elected by branches their names and addresses are given to those seeking the nomination. John Key went to visit them all, some more than once. One of those he visited twice was Garry Green at Kumeu. 'John came out and introduced himself. We just chewed the fat really. He was just so pleasant. Never once did he ask me to vote for him. I think he knew Brian Neeson had asked me to represent him.' Green soon had a dilemma.

> I knew Brian reasonably well. I used to introduce him to different people at the Rotary club and things like that, but John's potential hung out like the proverbial. He was clearly better. I had no doubt in my mind he

was Prime Minister material. I talked to some people and said, 'What the hell do I do?' A politician said to me, 'Vote for what you think is best for the country.'

He was not alone; he and another delegate debated what they should do. 'In the end we decided we've just got to do it – we switched our vote.'

Ten of Neeson's 38 switched, giving Key the nomination by just four votes. Had it not been for those like Garry Green who changed their votes that night, John Key might not be Prime Minister today. Key says now, 'If we hadn't won the selection in 2002 I thought I would try again in 2005, but I often wonder now whether I would have. It is more bruising and difficult than you think. It's pretty down and dirty.'

After losing the selection, Neeson decided to run as an independent. A series of procedural complaints kept the Helensville selection in the news from March until the election in July. The meeting had not started on time because one of the regional delegates could not find the venue, a little-known school in rural West Auckland, and regional chairman Scott Simpson had held proceedings up for 25 minutes until the Key voter arrived. 'Leaked' messages showed Boag had discouraged a third potential candidate from seeking selection for fear of splitting the vote. Boag was the usual villain of the stories, not Key, but they were a constant distraction to his first campaign.

National people blame Neeson for a story that appeared in the *Weekend Herald* of 29 June, on the subject of 'carpetbaggers', when the election campaign was under way. An item on candidates living outside the electorates they seek is a regular and legitimate feature of election coverage. The story by Bernard Orsman started: 'National Party candidate John Key is building a $5 million-plus home in Parnell about 20km away from the West Auckland seat of Helensville he is tipped to win.' The story was illustrated with a smiling Key in his painted campaign car and a smaller picture of the large house under construction in St Stephens Avenue. It also mentioned, along with a youthful mug shot, that 'Labour's Titirangi MP David Cunliffe who is standing in New Lynn at this election . . . now lives in Herne Bay on Marine Parade, one of the most exclusive streets in Auckland.'

The day the story appeared, Key was knocking on doors in Greenhithe.

> At one house a woman came to the door and said, 'You're that young guy in the paper building that big house in Parnell, aren't you?' I said, 'That's right.' She said, 'Are you a millionaire?' I went, 'Yep.' She said, 'Great, I'd never vote for anyone who hadn't made money.' I went next door, another beautiful home, knocked on the door, person answers, 'You're that young guy in the paper, aren't you?' And it was the complete opposite reaction. These things play out both ways.

Neeson's independent run was a greater problem. 'I knew I was in a little bit of trouble when I'd knock on doors and say I was the National candidate and they'd say, "No, Brian Neeson's the National candidate." They just didn't know, despite all the controversy there had been in the press.' Key estimates he knocked on about 10,000 doors in the electorate. Bronagh, Stephie and Max were out delivering leaflets too. The young ones were paid a cent for every house.

New candidates of Key's calibre, though, do not just

canvass their electorate. They make their arrival more widely known. He phoned me, among others in Auckland media no doubt, suggesting a chat. It is not unusual for editors and editorial writers to meet members of all political parties 'off the record', which means the politicians need not maintain the safe, certain postures of retail politics. You can get a sense from them of the uncertainties, complications, possibilities and personalities in public affairs. When he came in, John Key struck me as young, pleasant, polished by corporate success and out of touch with the country. When he left, I had the impression he must have been overseas for much longer than he was. He seemed not to have lived through the economic upheaval of the previous decades and showed no interest in it. He was clearly excited at the prospect of going to Parliament but I thought he had a lot of catching up to do.

On election day, 27 July, John Key won Helensville by 1589 votes. Neeson's majority in Waitakere had been 4056 in 1999. On paper, National's majority in the redrawn seat should have been nearer 6500. Neeson had split National's vote but it would have been down in any event. As the results came through on television it was a horror night for National. Nationwide, the party's share of the vote had fallen to 21 per cent, its lowest ever. It had gone into the election with 39 MPs and came out with just 27.

Recriminations raged in public for weeks and Boag took the blame, announcing she would not seek the presidency again. 'Better me than the leader,' she says now. But neither Bill English nor Michelle Boag nor anything the National Party had said or done in the previous three years was to blame. Opposition parties do not win elections, governments lose them, and Helen Clark had worked very hard to ensure her government would not lose this one. There was much more at stake for the Labour Party that year than she let on. It needed to win not just that election but also the next, to be a credible party of government again. The only Labour government in her lifetime to be re-elected even once had been the Lange–Douglas government, and most of Labour now disowned that one. The first Labour government of Savage and Fraser had lasted 14 years but came to an end before Clark and most current voters were born. The second, under Walter Nash, and the third, the Kirk–Rowling government, were each rejected after three years. Labour had been in power for only 12 of the previous 50 years. National had been the government far more often than not, throughout the second half of the twentieth century.

Clark's strategy for winning more than one election was perfectly attuned to the mood of a country that had been shaken by 15 years of rapid economic change. Hers was the first government since 1984 that had not set about reforms that had not been in its election manifesto. Clark's manifesto had been reduced to a small red card of promises her government could easily keep, and did. Thereafter, it had done nothing to surprise or seriously disturb anyone. Apart from raising the top rate of taxation and cancelling the Accident Compensation Corporation's exposure to competition, which had barely begun, the government did not reverse any of the economic reforms or extend them. The country was enjoying an export-led boom, with high commodity prices and an exchange rate that had fallen in response to Labour's election. Early in the term, Clark and Minister of Finance Michael Cullen became worried that business was antagonistic towards them and went out of their way to improve the relationship.

To project a sense of economic progress, they were looking to the British Labour government of Tony Blair for a post-Thatcherite, 'third way' idea – not quite hands-off, not quite picking winners. Clark adopted an Auckland University project, the 'Knowledge Wave', an exercise in infotech business consultancy that did not offer a coherent programme and struggled to survive the conference. No matter, New Zealand was enjoying the relief at last from so much economic reform and John Key took that lesson to heart.

National's problems at the 2002 election were also attributable to the election being the first under MMP at which voters were going to the polls knowing the government was practically certain to be returned. It was the first time people who normally vote National had a good reason to vote for one of the minor parties, and many did. A number voted for Peter Dunne's United Future team, not only because a television graphic, 'the worm', had turned every time he said 'common sense' in a debate, but because he was a potential coalition partner for Labour in its second term and might rescue it from the Greens. More than 60 per cent of voters for Dunne's party told a post-election *Herald*-DigiPoll survey that pre-election polls were the reason for their decision.

Just as many cast a vote for ACT, and even more for New Zealand First. Each of those parties received a far higher proportion of the vote than they normally enjoy. United Future's eight seats gave Helen Clark an alternative governing partner to the Greens and she happily accepted it. The Greens were driving a hard line against genetic engineering of crops, an issue that had nearly derailed her election campaign when TV3 surprised her with some engineered corn. Dunne did a soft deal for Labour's second term and the Greens were marginalised.

The new MP for Helensville, meanwhile, had a post-election question to answer. Taking the 'carpetbagger' charge too seriously, he had bought a property in the electorate and believed that it had permitted him to vote there. Was it his 'primary place of residence' as required by the Electoral Act? He and Bronagh were living in Arney Road, Remuera while waiting for the St Stephens Avenue house to be finished. But the Electoral Act defines a primary place of residence as one that carries an emotional attachment and Key was looking forward to the lifestyle block they had bought at Waimauku. The plan was to live out there at weekends. Bronagh liked the idea of land where the kids, having grown up in London with no lawn, could run around. The property had duck ponds and fields. It was beautiful.

John consulted lawyer and National MP Richard Worth who advised that the property would allow them to vote in the electorate. Political opponents were not so sure. The issue soon faded but the weekend house did not work out. 'After a while,' says Key, 'we found the kids had sport and other things going on in the city at weekends. It was a hassle to pack everything and go out there. In the end we thought, "Do people really care whether I'm living in the electorate?"' When they decided to sell it he went to the suburban paper the *Western Leader* and asked them to put it on the front page so everybody knew. Nobody seemed to mind. These days he has the biggest majority in the country, 'because I am Prime Minister and it is a National seat'.

He holds a clinic in Helensville once a month. Two

secretaries at his electorate office ensure only genuine constituents get through the door. Trade association lobbyists and the like sometimes try to see him there.

> To be honest, I don't think I am the best electorate MP in the world. I wish I had more time for constituents. The trade-off is I can get things for them – I probably have greater influence – though I am careful with approaches to people like the immigration minister. I tell them [ministers], 'I will write to you with what I think is a genuine case but you have to make the same decision you would for anyone else.'

He insists he has had ministers turn his cases down, including immigration cases that are handled by a minister who is usually lowly ranked.

Looking back, Michelle Boag thinks it was crucial that Key secured an electorate seat.

> It is very important for a leader to have that sort of moral authority. On all sides of the House, it is much better for them to have an electorate. Helensville was a good seat and a getting-better seat. He did do the hard yards, did knock on doors, all the retail stuff. Never at any stage did you get the feeling that he thought he was better than that and shouldn't have to do it. Our problem in 2002 was, there were not enough MPs retiring. In 1990 we had such a big intake and it wasn't properly controlled because nobody thought we would get that many in. It was before MMP. So we got all

these MPs who stuck around and were never going to make cabinet.

Not enough retirements at each election is not a problem National has faced on Key's watch. As the 2014 election approached, no fewer than 15 National MPs were retiring or had left Parliament since the previous election. Mindful perhaps of the battle of Helensville, he has actively encouraged some to consider doing what he had done: try a second career.

CHAPTER EIGHT

Rapid Rise

All MPs remember their maiden speech. It is their proudest moment, the only speech they might make in the House when no other member interjects and some even pay attention. New members invite their families to Parliament for the occasion.

Walking along the corridors, past the portraits and the paintings, feeling the heritage, the importance and the prestige, John Key's sister Sue said, 'This is awesome.'

Key turned to her and laughed. 'You were the one who said, "Don't do it!"'

It was true. When he had decided to go into politics he had taken them all to a family conference at Hanmer Springs: Liz and Roger and their daughter Milly, Sue and her two boys, Tim and Riley, and John's family. They knew he had never lost that childhood ambition, but when it came to the point, Sue had said, 'Why do you want to go into politics? Nobody likes politicians. Why can't you run Air New Zealand or something?' She had not been inside Parliament Buildings then. It is 'awesome', as she put it. 'There is an aura there, a system and order, and it is beautiful. Parliament is lovely. He had his name on the door.'

Members love it, staff love it, the press gallery loves it. Even the House, meaning the debating chamber, for all its petty points of order, pompous procedure, occasional nasty exchanges and usually tedious speeches, is loveable. It is a place where the political tribes meet across a narrow aisle, eye to eye, and despite the tension and antagonism, the dignity of the House always prevails. It is an arena that civilises a political mind. Fiercely driven people from both sides of politics go to Parliament on a mission to confront evil and, once there, find they are facing people who are not the devils they imagined but people with whom they have something in common: they care for the same country.

Maiden speeches follow a standard format: gratitude to voters and vital supporters, a description of the electorate's features and problems, a tribute to the previous MP – which John Key managed to do, though not before noting he was 'the only member of the National caucus to have beaten a National candidate to get here'. Every new MP acknowledges their family and important influences. 'My views on life were shaped by a remarkable woman: my late mother, Ruth,' said Key. She was 'living testimony that one gets out of life what one puts into it. There is no substitute for hard work and determination. Those are the attitudes she instilled in me.'

His seat was in the back row of the opposition benches. National's five new MPs were ranked in alphabetical order and Key came after Brash, Collins, Brian Connell (Rakaia) and Sandra Goudie (Coromandel). Brash in fact had a front-row seat, going straight into Parliament as the party's finance spokesman. Key was the last-ranked

MP if you excluded Maurice Williamson who had been banished to the back of the room, not for the first or last time in his long career. He had publicly blamed National's poor election result on Michelle Boag and by implication the dissension her 'dead wood' drive had created in Helensville.

From his seat at the back, Key concentrated on watching and learning the mysterious rules and procedures of the House. One afternoon early in the term, he was listening to ACT leader Richard Prebble, a veteran down in front, as Prebble argued with the Speaker about the way a Labour minister was proposing to advance a bill. Prebble pressed his point and the Speaker agreed with him, telling the minister he would have to go about the legislation in a different way. National's Gerry Brownlee, who had agreed to the government's desired procedure, was glaring at him. When the debate moved on, the ACT leader was surprised to be quietly joined at his bench by the new member for Helensville who whispered, 'I'm curious, what did you just do?' Prebble was impressed.

> Nobody in the National Party had ever asked me what I had done on a point of order. So I explained the point and how it worked. Then he asked me, 'Why did you do it?' I told him the government had been setting a trap and the Nats were walking right into it. If we had gone along with it we'd have found we couldn't move an amendment to the bill. Now the issue would go to a committee and we could look at it. The point was actually complex but I could tell from what he went on to ask me that he grasped it immediately. About 70 per cent of MPs retire without ever understanding these things. He is quick.

Roger Norton, Ruth's boarder at Hollyford Avenue when John was starting high school, went into the public gallery at Parliament to watch the man whose plans and progress Ruth had so often mentioned. Key was in the chamber, and when he realised Norton was in the gallery, came up to see him.

'John,' said Norton, 'isn't this a lot of rubbish?'

'There are games that get played in here and you do your dues,' replied Key. 'We get the work done but we could do it quicker.'

'Haven't you got something better to do?' Norton asked.

'No,' said Key, 'I think I can make a difference.'

———————

Most who enter Parliament share that motive to 'make a difference' and politics can be cruel to the best of them. National's incoming 'class of 2002' got to see just how cruel it could be. The day they arrived for their first caucus meeting, brimming with first-day excitement, they walked into a wake. No fewer than 16 of the previous caucus were there to be farewelled. Only six had planned to retire. Jenny Shipley, Wyatt Creech, Max Bradford, John Luxton, Doug Kidd and Warren Kyd were given silver trays. The other 10 had seen their careers disappear that Saturday night. Gavan Herlihy, who had thought his Otago seat safe, said to reporters, 'Six years ago I wandered up those steps with such hope in my heart. Today the heart is . . .' He didn't want to blame anyone. He turned away with an audible 'bugger'.

Timing is everything in a political career. The right moment to come into Parliament is not when your chosen party is in power or even coming to power. New Zealand has seen political figures such as Jim McLay and Jim

Anderton who had all the qualities of a prime minister and almost certainly would have made it to the top if they had entered Parliament at a different time. The right moment is when the party is at its lowest ebb. When John Key decided to make the jump from finance to politics, he chose the perfect year.

National MPs detest being in opposition. Labour MPs do not relish it either, but more of them appear to enjoy political debate. National MPs go into politics to run the country, not to spend all their time talking about it. They wanted this second term in opposition to be their last and none of them was more impatient than a new MP who was getting on in years, Don Brash. Within nine months of the election, Brash was clearly planning to challenge English for the leadership. He accepted an invitation to address that year's conference of the ACT Party where he was greeted by the party's president as the 'ninth ACT MP'. He used his speech to criticise National's 'spectacular lack of success', which brought a pointed response from Gerry Brownlee who also had higher aspirations. 'If people in the National Party think we are going to increase the National vote by saying we are inextricably linked to ACT,' Brownlee growled, 'then they have got their heads so far into the sand all they can expect is for their backsides to be kicked at the next election.' ACT in fact had helped National in Helensville at the election, deciding not to stand a candidate in case Key's vote was split three ways, handing the seat to Labour.

Amid all the dissension, Helensville's new MP kept his head down. He, too, was already touted as a future leader, but that has never been a guarantee anyone would get there. English had carried that mantle since arriving in Parliament, as had another who was sitting on the front bench, Rangitikei's Simon Power. With such a crowded field it was better for a newcomer to bide his time. His electorate and his assigned policy area, transport, were giving Key enough to do for the moment.

Labour was planning to take the air force away from Whenuapai and put state houses into a mixed residential development on surplus land at the Hobsonville base. An MP who had grown up in a state house with better-off housing nearby could have been expected to see the benefits of 'pepper potting' state tenancies. With good design the rental properties might be indistinguishable from the owned homes next door and tenants might do their utmost to see that there was no visible distinction. But the new MP sided with constituents whose vision of state housing was of run-down neighbourhoods, though he did not oppose the project in those terms. He argued the land was too valuable and Housing New Zealand should capitalise it to build more state houses somewhere else. He was already learning to smooth away the rough edge of any position he would take.

The Whenuapai air base presented him with a more delicate political issue. Quite a number of his better-off constituents and those in National electorates north of the Auckland harbour bridge liked a proposal supported by the mayors of Waitakere, North Shore and Rodney to turn Whenuapai into a commercial airport. For frequent business travellers to Wellington from the North Shore or the Hibiscus Coast, a drive to nearby Whenuapai was a great deal more attractive than the journey through the city to Mangere. However, for many of Key's constituents in the developing suburbs of the northwest, and many on the Shore living under Whenuapai's flight path, the prospect was much less appealing.

Given such strong constituencies for both views, the local MP could have gone either way. He adopted a position based on practicalities. 'The Whenuapai runway is built of hexagonal concrete blocks designed specifically to stand up to bombing,' he wrote in the *Herald*. 'This is ideal for military purposes but it would provide a bumpy landing for ordinary planes.' Upgrading the runway would cost $70 million, and even with it, the airfield could not accommodate jumbo jets. The area around the airport would not be enough for the shopping, car parking, fuel storage and ancillary industries that provided Mangere with the bulk of its revenue, even if a second commercial airport could attract them, which he doubted. Auckland's second airport was eventually defeated at local elections.

Free 'conscience' votes in Parliament pose a particular challenge for new MPs still establishing themselves in an electorate. They tend to surrender their personal view to constituents. Key faced two free votes in his first term: a bill to legalise prostitution; and, later, a civil union bill giving partners of the same sex a right to marry in all but name. Key's usual view of these things is liberal, an outlook he attributes to his mother's influence. Ruth had a European attitude to subjects such as teenage smoking and social behaviour. Her children were trusted to make their own decisions and take responsibility for the consequences.

At an early stage in the passage of the Prostitution Reform Bill, Key told the House he intended to support it. 'I do not believe, and will never believe,' he declared, 'that the government can legislate for morality.' He calculated that with about 8000 sex workers in New Zealand, each with an average of three clients a night, there must be 100,000 people going to brothels, '10 per cent of the current population of eligible men in New Zealand'. He doubted the bill would make any difference to that number. But when it came to its final reading he voted against it. He did not speak at the final stage. He told the press he had decided in the end that the bill sent the wrong message. He also voted against civil unions, as did all National MPs in 2004 except Katherine Rich, Clem Simich and Pansy Wong. Yet just eight years later, as Prime Minister, Key's voice was probably pivotal to the public acceptance of Labour MP Louisa Wall's same-sex marriage bill when he declared he was not opposed to it.

The political issue that shook the country most in his first year in Parliament came out of nowhere and took all sides by surprise. The country's best judicial minds, sitting as the Court of Appeal and soon to become its Supreme Court, issued a decision that declared the tidal foreshore and the seabed beyond could be still in Maori ownership. The ruling overturned law as it had been understood for more than a century. Acts of Parliament, the court found, had not expunged customary native title which, unlike English concepts of real estate, could extend beyond dry land.

The court had not ruled Maori did own foreshore and seabed, merely that the claim in the case it had heard could be considered. But the door had been opened and the implications seemed obvious. The public might no longer be able to freely use all beaches. A central value of New Zealand life appeared to be at stake. Labour quickly decided it could not let the ruling stand. National was no less anxious, urging the government to assert public ownership by legislation. All parties except the Greens and one or two Maori MPs, notably Labour's Tariana Turia, wanted the decision overturned. Public alarm was palpable and ran deep but it did not immediately hurt the government in the polls or boost National's numbers. National was still polling an abysmal 26.8 per cent in a *Herald*-DigiPoll survey of August 2003, more than a year after the election.

The days were darkening for Bill English's leadership and early in October he moved to pre-empt a challenge from Brash. Having lined up enough support, he thought, English called a vote a few days before the weekly caucus meeting where the challenge was expected. The ploy failed and Brash emerged from the party room its new leader. When Brash reallocated opposition speaking roles he kept finance for himself but made John Key an associate finance spokesman. Key's vote was one of those English had counted on. When English saw the new MP promoted so quickly to a finance role it would have made him suspect he had been misled. Yet while Brash gave Key a speaking role that Key's credentials could hardly deny him, Brash left him on the backbench. Key has since said he voted for English that day.

> I voted for Bill. No one believes me. I'm not 100 per cent sure to this day that Bill believes me, but the reason I didn't vote for Don was I knew he was really, really, really right wing, and I thought, 'How do you win an election when you are at the fringe of the party's support?' You are hugely loved by those people but in the world of MMP, we have to get virtually half the population to like us.

For all that, Brash made a difference. In the New Year of 2004, he used a 'state of the nation' address to the Orewa Rotary Club to launch a frontal assault on the idea that

Maori had a distinctive place in the affairs of New Zealand. Maori, Brash noted, were now all of mixed blood. The nation was one people. The Treaty of Waitangi had been taken out of its historic context and was being used to divide New Zealanders. Policy was making one race a privileged group. Maori were no different from Pacific Islanders or other non-Maori on welfare. It was, he thought, 'bizarre that, in a society where the Prime Minister refuses to allow grace to be said at a state banquet, because, she says, we are an increasingly secular society, we fly Maori elders around the world to lift tapu and expel evil spirits from New Zealand embassies'. When Maori had to be consulted for resource consents, they were 'inventing or rediscovering beliefs for pecuniary gain' in a way that was 'becoming deeply corrupt' and looking like 'standover tactics'.

The speech struck a resoundingly popular chord in the wake of the foreshore and seabed controversy. Talkback radio and letters to the editor hailed Brash for saying what many had previously been reluctant to say out loud. National had an immediate bump in the polls. The positions of the major parties turned completely around, National jumping to 45 per cent to Labour's 38 per cent. In an effort to stem the damage, Helen Clark announced an inquiry into the place of the Treaty in New Zealand, and another to review policies for Maori to ensure they were based on need, not 'privilege'. But inside the National Party, long-standing Maori members Wira Gardiner and his wife Hekia Parata were reviewing their continued membership. Parata said she was 'ashamed' of the speech: 'It's the antithesis of everything I've worked for professionally and personally.' National's sole Maori MP, Georgina te Heuheu, said it was 'an extremely different tack to the National Party I entered Parliament with'. Brash suggested she resign as his spokeswoman for Maori affairs.

The backlash against Maori rights blew out within a year. The more lasting and significant consequence of the foreshore and seabed debate was Tariana Turia's departure from the Labour Party to form a Maori Party co-led by a prominent cultural figure, Dr Pita Sharples. John Key, meanwhile, was quietly going to Waitangi. His mentor there was Dame Jenny Shipley who continued to observe the national day at Waitangi after leaving office. As Prime Minister in 1998–99, Shipley had worked hard to help the host marae create a constructive annual commemoration of the Treaty. Previous prime ministers had stopped going to the Treaty grounds after indignities perpetrated by protesters every year.

Shipley encouraged the hosts to hold an open forum at Te Tii marae on the day before 6 February, where the chiefs of 1840 had debated on the day before they made the Treaty. She and her ministers sat under a marquee and listened all day to whatever people wanted to say. Opposition leader Helen Clark was listening too and not impressed. She did not attend the forum, or even Waitangi most years, when she became Prime Minister. But the talking at Te Tii has continued and Waitangi offers all parliamentarians a day on which they might feel the pulse of an indigenous culture. Shipley says Key felt it.

> Before he became leader, though it was clear to me he was going to be, I made the offer I make to every National leader. I said to John if he would like to just wander around with me up there I could share some of the contacts and insights I've gained. He came. I remember him standing in that lower marae area saying, 'I had no idea all this existed. I understand I will have to come to grips with this.'

CHAPTER NINE

'Crony Capitalist'

John Key had been the talk of Auckland business circles since he entered politics. The question being asked with increasing urgency after he became a National finance spokesman in 2004 was 'What does he stand for?' The question really meant, 'What did he believe a government's role in the economy should be?'

By 2004, Helen Clark's government was reaping the benefits of high commodity export prices, rising house prices, and levels of unemployment which had fallen to a point where labour shortages were appearing. National's new finance spokesman believed the economy should be doing even better and his background gave him credibility when he reckoned he could take it to a higher level. In interviews he talked of making a 'step change'. He often said, if New Zealand was a company he would buy it but would increase its 'gearing'. He dared say – or at least did not deny – that he believed the public accounts could carry more debt.

It was 20 years since the advent of 'Rogernomics', 10 years since inflation had been beaten, eight years since the budget was last in deficit. New Zealand's public policy was practically textbook. The economy was like a garden that had been cleared of its tangle of subsidies, tax incentives, restrictive licensing and most other political influences. It was an open market for 'a thousand flowers to bloom', but precious few new shoots were appearing in the private sector.

Those listening to Key at corporate lunches were by no means of one mind on what more should be done. They nodded when Roger Kerr of the Business Roundtable held to the line that governments should not favour particular industries. Kerr urged ever more reductions in government spending, which would allow the Reserve Bank to hold its interest rate and that could possibly lower the dollar's exchange rate for the benefit of exports. They also nodded, more cautiously, when some corporate voices advocated more active government in partnerships with business. 'New Zealand Inc.', they called it. Critics of both the left and right dubbed it 'crony capitalism'.

Crony capitalism is not corruption, at least not in New Zealand. The term refers to the innocent damage that a government can do to its economy when it provides selective favours to certain industries or projects that would not need the favour if they were economic. They would attract sufficient private investment if they were profitable. Too much crony capitalism will leave too much of the economy generating too little value, which is what had happened by 1984.

No government since then had withdrawn industry support entirely. Grants for research and development continued. One or two industries, notably film production, had even convinced successive governments to grant them tax favours, arguing that they generated wider economic benefits. The Labour government was assisting software investments and, less successfully, a boat-builder, Sovereign Yachts, which had plans to set up at Hobsonville. But these were exceptions to the prevailing rule. When it came to public finance, business had learned not to ask. Might John Key be different?

Key was hard to read because, unlike all other leading figures in politics, he had no history. He had not been in politics in the 1980s or 1990s. He had not even joined the National Party until around 1998. If he had any views on what had been done in those decades, he gave no hint of them in speeches. He was determined to turn his back on National's unpopular government of the 1990s and treated the whole era as though it had never happened. Most political commentators at the time were assuming that because Key had made a fortune in a finance market he was a rampant free marketeer beneath the bland, moderate language of his speeches. But business audiences were less sure. He had no reason to hide his true beliefs from them.

In his maiden speech to Parliament, he had extolled the active government role in the economies of two countries in which he had worked: Singapore and Ireland. He harboured an early hope that New Zealand might become an international base for back-office services to banks, much as Ireland had become. In an interview shortly before the 2005 election he gave the *Herald*'s Fran O'Sullivan an enthusiastic account of Irish co-operation with Merrill Lynch. The Irish Development Agency people used to attend Merrill board meetings, he told her, and come up with ideas to help the company and adjust rules if necessary, 'as long as it was not intended to thwart the opposition'. He had shifted a great deal of Merrill's London business to Dublin where the tax rate for foreign companies was 10 per cent. 'We transferred across the aircraft leasing business, the complex interest rates derivatives business, the entire back office for global foreign exchange and a huge chunk of private clients' business.'

The Irish model was, 'the complete opposite of the way we operate in New Zealand at the moment – the government sector was much more interactive, much more user-friendly, much more industry-based and less focused on grants'. Ireland was called a 'tiger' economy at that time. Its banking problems and its euro crisis were still some years off. Key admired not just its tax concessions but its public investment in a national broadband network. When it came to building 'infrastructure', Key was an enthusiast for so-called public–private partnerships.

'PPPs', if properly designed, give the public the benefit of commercial investors' assessment of a project that a government believes to be worthwhile. The benefit depends on whether the PPP exposes the private partner to the risk of losing money if its assessment is astray. John Key did not quite see it that way. Early in his parliamentary career he attacked a government bill on transport development, blaming the Greens for imposing too tough a test on PPPs. The bill would mean, he wrote, 'no road can be built unless its projected toll income guarantees its self-sufficiency'. He contrasted that with schemes in Australia, England and much of Europe where governments underwrote a minimum level of revenue for the private partner or provided operating subsidies until the toll income is sufficient. This, he said, enabled tolls to be set 'at less than economic rates, so motorists are actively encouraged to use the new road'.

Later, as party leader, he committed National to laying fibre-optic cable for ultra-fast broadband throughout the country at an up-front cost to the taxpayer of $1.5 billion. When he first floated that idea in 2007, his deputy Bill English doubted its wisdom on the grounds that it would 'crowd out' private-sector investment. In Australia the Rudd Labor government was planning a similar network to criticism from former Liberal Prime Minister John Howard. Howard insisted it was a decision that should be made by the private sector. Key considered the subject to be a case of 'market failure', meaning unless all providers of cable could build a new network at the same time, it would not happen. Or at least it would not happen fast enough for New Zealand to take full advantage of telecommunications developments. This was infrastructure too important to wait for the private sector to meet a demand. The supply would create the demand.

Key was a worry for those who remembered the 'think big' schemes of earlier governments. What Key thought about those, and indeed all the government initiatives deemed wise at one time, he never said. If he was obliged to give a speech reflecting on events of the past, or wanted to source a political heritage for himself, he reached back to the governments of Sidney Holland and Keith Holyoake, who stepped down when Key was aged 10.

He managed to deliver a speech in honour of Jenny Shipley in 2006 without once mentioning her role as social welfare minister in the 1991 benefit 'cuts', which reduced standard benefits by a quarter and put the money into allowances for specific needs. It was one of the few elements of Ruth Richardson's 'mother of all budgets' that has endured to this day. The 1991 budget helped bring inflation down rapidly and put public finances on course for a surplus – a word not heard for as long as anyone could remember. Richardson and the budget were not mentioned either. Shipley completely understands Key's position.

> He doesn't talk about these things and nor should he. We stand on the shoulders of others. He couldn't do what he is doing if we hadn't done what we had to do, and I wouldn't wish them to have to do it again. It was demanding and he doesn't need to go back and drag it up.

But history is not a closed book. A Prime Minister's perspective on his country's recent experience is vitally important. Here, possibly for the first time, is John Key's view of where we have been.

> Effectively, New Zealand was an offshoot of the British economy, Britain's larder, which completely changed in the 1970s. We had what was normal and orthodox for its day: highly unionised markets, restricted borders, controlled exchange rate, all of those things. Because we were a small economy we were always less able to stand severe shocks and then we got two: Britain's entry to Europe and the oil crisis. We might have been able to handle one but we certainly couldn't handle both. The rigidity of those policy settings didn't allow the economy to adjust.
>
> I never met Muldoon. I've read stuff about him but I don't know everything that went on. I remember reading [*Rise and Fall of a*] *Young Turk* at school. I suspect Muldoon was a really bright guy, probably quite savvy. As things turned to custard and he had to respond, there were two pathways he could have

taken. One was to liberalise the economy, which would have been brave given that most economies were not liberalising then, or really try and manually intervene and adjust – and of course he did that, beyond the point where it was rational actually.

Muldoon went through wage-price freezes and all sorts of crazy things, and the economy was ground to a point of hopelessness both from a competitiveness and from an innovation perspective. Essentially by 1984 we were broke. So I think [Labour's] reforms were right. A problem may have been the pace of them, but once you are doing these things you keep going.

The pace of change was a lot to absorb in a short time. They were doing a binary switch and I think there is a path somewhere in the middle. You saw it in the wine industry. We were producing terrible wine and they opened up the wine industry but it was one area where they were a bit more rational. They paid people to take out the old vines and start growing new ones with a bit of government support in there. Whereas with the other things, SMPs [supplementary minimum prices for farm products], it was a case of 'Bad luck, you're on your own and we hope it will come right'.

Before the '87 crash it was going well, people were doing quite well. But I think what really killed Lange was that the changes were always going to have an effect on lower-income and very unskilled people. That, in the end, was who he represented. As he lost confidence, Douglas grew in confidence and they were going in different directions.

At times when we were in the dealing room, and Brash would have been Reserve Bank governor, unemployment was quite high, and I remember us sitting around thinking, 'You can't possibly do this. How can you be so stupid as to raise interest rates when unemployment is so high?' But ultimately he had only one thing to measure and that was inflation in the band, not other factors. I don't know whether it was too fast. I think the issue came more with the 1990–93 stuff when the voters did vote for a slowdown and that actually didn't happen. Maybe they [National] were right. In the end, all of that economic policy has been good for New Zealand.

Painless, publicly imperceptible reform is hard to sustain. Key annoys some of those who saw the courage of politicians at that time when he privately refers to their reforms as 'low-hanging fruit'. He says he does not mean to suggest it was easy to float the dollar, remove import licensing, expose manufacturing to competition, but rather that these sweeping changes were easy to understand by comparison with the dull programme of incremental economic improvements since.

The man who was 'so stupid' as to raise interest rates in the 1991–92 recession led National into the 2005 election. The party's manifesto under Don Brash was not very brave. It promised tax cuts at all levels, though it kept Labour's 39 cents per dollar top rate for incomes above $100,000 lest it was accused of favouring the rich. It dared not nominate spending cuts to balance the loss of tax. It also, Key points out, promised no change to the terms of national superannuation – a position Brash condemns when Key adheres to it today.

Labour was so worried about the tax cuts that Helen Clark went into the first television debate with Don Brash visibly pumped and proceeded to shout him down every time he mentioned the subject. Afterwards, Brash told the press he finds it difficult to debate fiercely with a woman, which made matters worse for him. Deputy Prime Minister Michael Cullen attempted a similar tactic in television's finance debate but Key proved more than a match. To counter the appeal of National's tax cuts, Labour announced mid-campaign that if elected it would wipe interest charges on student loans for the duration of study.

The economic debate, however, was overshadowed in the final week by questions about Brash's dealings with an obscure religious sect, the Exclusive Brethren, who had been circulating scare pamphlets against the Greens and Labour. Brash at first denied knowing who was behind the pamphlets, then, when the seven-man group came forward, issued a public apology for his denial. He admitted he had met the sect up to four times in the previous 18 months, and that at the most recent meeting they had told him they would be producing pamphlets. He apologised in particular to his deputy Gerry Brownlee and other colleagues for not telling them what he knew, causing Brownlee to make false statements on National Radio. When opponents called him a liar he denied it in terms that produced the disastrous headline: 'Brash: I'm not a liar'. The saga was classic Brash, starting from an artless admission of something that need not have become an issue. A better politician would have shrugged at the pamphlets and told opponents and critics to harden up. None of it probably made much difference to voters' intentions.

The racial backlash Brash had fomented the previous year still simmered in the background, reinforced by divided billboards contrasting 'iwi' with 'kiwi', and the election-night count was very close. National doubled its 2002 result, taking back votes from ACT, United Future and New Zealand First to reach 39 per cent, its best result since 1990 and just short of Labour's 41 per cent. Helen Clark went into her third term on support agreements with Winston Peters and Peter Dunne, but Brash was not in immediate danger. He had brought National back to within a whisker of victory. He and Brownlee were re-elected leader and deputy at the party's first post-election caucus, now swelled by 23 new MPs. At a press conference afterward, the 65-year-old agreed that he had indicated he would step down if defeated at the election but had changed his mind. 'I can see myself fighting the next election, certainly,' he said.

A month later, in the first post-election poll, Colmar Brunton had National up five points on its election result, four ahead of Labour, though Brash's personal support was down to 24 per cent and the party's finance spokesman, widely praised for his campaign performance, had entered the 'preferred Prime Minister' rankings with 5 per cent. Some in the party put the word around the press gallery that Brash might not have meant to be categorical about staying on. But when the question was put to him again, he confirmed he was continuing.

In the last poll of the year, Key had risen two more points, Brash had dropped further and National had lengthened its lead. Reviewing 2005, *Herald* political commentator John Armstrong wrote:

> Key has delivered the standout performance of the year. He has hardly put a foot wrong. He is the first National MP to get the better of Cullen in Parliament...

He ends the year snapping at Brash's heels in the preferred Prime Minister stakes . . . Key's success is in part down to obvious intellect, unrelenting drive, superb communication skills and absence of self-doubt. The competence and self-confidence makes it easy to forget how far he has come in little more than three years in Parliament.

CHAPTER TEN

Rebranding National

Don Brash was not a natural in Parliament. He would stand woodenly and read from notes. But his members thought he was doing better in September 2006, leading their attack on the government's use of public funds for its 'pledge card' at the previous year's election, and the personal favours a prospective immigrant had done for Labour MP Taito Phillip Field. The opposition was using the two issues to try to taint the government with a charge of 'corruption' and Helen Clark had had enough. If it was war that National wanted, she told the media, war it would get. The next day in Parliament when the opposition leader stood to ask the first question, Trevor Mallard fired the bullet. Brash, his interjection implied, was having an affair.

Never quick on his feet, Brash stopped dead. Long seconds passed before he regrouped and started the question. 'Did the Prime Minister's handling of the Taito Phillip Field affair show that . . .'

'Speaking of affairs,' interjected Mallard again.

Brash looked beseechingly to the chair. Speaker Margaret Wilson asked Mallard to 'contain himself' but the damage was done.

A few days later Brash issued a press release in Auckland that his marriage was having difficulties and he was taking leave from Parliament. He was not away long but there was no coming back. National had been enjoying a healthy lead in the polls which immediately turned against it.

Brash eventually stepped down in November amid another drama, this time leaving a false impression he was forced to resign by a book – *The Hollow Men* – based on his personal email log. He obtained a blanket court injunction against publication of his private messages, until author Nicky Hager indicated he was interested only in political disclosures, nothing personal. Brash agreed to limit the injunction so that the book could be published. By the time it appeared he had resigned.

Brash has said he told Key as early as 2004, when they shared a motel in Blenheim, that win or lose the election, he would hand over to Key within the next term of Parliament. Key remembers the conversation and did not take it too seriously.

> I never took it as a Tony Blair–Gordon Brown deal, a John Howard–Peter Costello thing. On numerous occasions he told me he believed I was his natural successor. But if he had won the election, I couldn't have walked in around 2007 and said, 'Time to honour the commitment.' It wasn't like that.

The caucus would elect a new leader on Monday, 27 November. Key was nearly certain to win but there were other possibilities. Bill English, a year younger than Key, had been in Parliament much longer – 16 years, having arrived at the age of 28. He had taken the party leadership at a bad time, lost it after an unwinnable election and now he wanted it again. English believed Key was not ready, not sufficiently well established in National's culture to represent the party as effectively as English could. It was not a particularly convincing case and English did not push it very far. On the Sunday before the vote, Key, English, Murray McCully and Simon Power gathered at Key's Parnell home. English would be deputy leader if Gerry Brownlee could be persuaded to stand aside. Brownlee had been deputy to Brash and was not about to go down with the leader. But over the weekend Brownlee relented. On the Sunday afternoon, the 'dream team' for caucus unity was agreed.

At the caucus meeting next day, Key was elected leader, English deputy. It was a 'whirlwind day', Key recalls.

> When you win, the enormity of it hits you, and you realise lots of people are relying on you to get this right. That's the big thing you feel when you become the leader. It is not just the caucus but the party and all the activists and supporters – they are all relying on you.

He walked out of the caucus side by side with English to do the press conference, a round of television interviews, and take calls from well-wishers and media around the country. A Nelson radio station, Fresh FM, wanted him for some quick-fire questions: 'Did man land on the moon?' 'What's your position on abortion?' 'Were you for or against the tour?' To the last Key responded, 'Nineteen eighty-one? I don't really know. It's such a long time ago'. It was pay dirt for the Labour Party, calling into question the credibility of National's new leader.

Key's first speech as leader was given to a party luncheon at North Harbour Stadium. 'On many occasions,' he began, 'I have read in the media that John Key did a good job against Michael Cullen at the last election, that John Key knows his stuff on finance, but that no one knows what John Key really stands for.' What followed was a paean to family values, hard work, education, the social welfare system – 'you can measure a society by how it looks after its most vulnerable; once I was one of them . . .' – and his desire to encourage personal aspirations. On economics, he said: 'I am interested in what works and not what should, or could, or might work in theory. I do not intend to follow an ideological path without ever challenging the concept or considering its appropriateness in our unique New Zealand setting.'

But when he turned to the country's ethnic mix, the new leader gave only a passing nod to Brash who was in the audience. 'While there is only one New Zealand, it is made up of people of many backgrounds . . . the National Party will always believe in one standard of citizenship and I want to make this very clear to you today.' Then he adopted a theme National Party members had not heard from their leader for a while.

> Maori are the tangata whenua of this country and we have nothing to fear by acknowledging that. It is part of what makes New Zealand unique. I welcome the Maori renaissance and some of the great initiatives like the kohanga reo movement which have come from Maori, for Maori. It is encouraging to see Maori using

the resources they have to help address the obstacles that are standing in the way of their young people achieving their potential.

Near the end he came to social welfare, and used a word – 'underclass' – that would define his first months as leader.

> It is in the interests of no one, and to the shame of us all, that an underclass has been allowed to develop in New Zealand. This underclass is represented by all ethnic backgrounds, and when I talk about lifting people's sights I am talking about all New Zealanders. It is not the New Zealand way, and if left to fester it will impinge on us all. My party is deadly serious about addressing these issues.

He returned to the subject in his first 'state of the nation' speech in early 2007, at a venue he knew well, the Burnside Rugby Club in Christchurch. He had played junior rugby at the club and later, more seriously, played squash there. It was close to his old school and not far from the state house he grew up in. The proximity suited his subject.

> Since I've been an MP, I've talked to a lot of people who grew up in my street or in streets like it. Many have done well for themselves. However, things are different now than they were 30 years ago. It used to be that any street in any community could be the launching pad for a happy and fulfilling life. That is not the case any more. Today many are being left behind. There are streets in our country where helplessness has become ingrained, [where] people believe they are locked out of everyday New Zealand, and are locked into a way

of life for which the exit signs and the road maps have long since been discarded.

I'm not just talking about poor communities, because we all know being poor needn't rob you of hope. I'm talking about places where the rungs on the ladder of opportunity have been broken. I'm talking about streets like McGehan Close in Owairaka, Auckland. In one week last year, two kids in that small street killed themselves and another two made unsuccessful attempts. It is a street terrorised by youth gangs. Around the country, there are other places like this. The worst are home to families that have been jobless for more than one generation, families destroyed by alcohol and P addiction, where there is nothing more to read than a pizza flyer, families who send their kids to school with empty stomachs and empty lunch boxes and Mum and kids live in fear of another beating from Dad.

The speech sent Auckland reporters racing to McGehan Close. There, machine operator Jason Thompson (27) told the *Herald*, 'That's all shit. There's worse underclass streets than this. We had a hanging [suicide] here last year but these things happen on any streets, even in rich neighbourhoods.'

'I don't think what he said is fair,' said part-time Salvation Army truck driver Charlie Pulu. 'We have a clean street and people are kind here.'

'I think he's all shit,' said Joan Nathan. 'He should come down here and see for himself. Just because we go to Housing Corp and that and ask for help we get turned down, but if an immigrant goes there and has money, they're in.'

Learning that resident gangs used the playground at the top of the street, the reporters met six teenage boys there.

'Who are you, bro, and what are you doing here talking to these people?' one demanded. 'Are you talking about us?'

His breath smelled of alcohol and he cradled a box of beer under one arm. The reporters estimated he was no older than 16.

At Parliament, Key's speech threw the Labour government off balance. Helen Clark insisted the 'underclass' was shrinking and issued figures in support. Minister of Education Steve Maharey said 'social outcomes are improving dramatically'. Key invited Clark to accompany him to McGehan Close which was so close to her electorate it used to be in it. Clark issued a curt reply.

'The Prime Minister is a regular visitor to low-decile schools and communities and doesn't require his company. However, she recognises it may be a unique experience for him.'

Key went to McGehan Close that weekend as Joan Nathan had challenged him to, met her 12-year-old daughter Aroha and invited the girl to accompany him to Waitangi in a few days' time for Waitangi Day celebrations. Key also announced he had contacted a Te Atatu cereal supplier to arrange free breakfast for the nearby Wesley Primary School as the beginning of a national food in schools programme. An annoyed principal, Rae Parkin, said the school did not need it. Some kids did come to school hungry, she said, but she had seen hungry children at her previous school, a decile eight (near the top of the social scale).

Aroha went to Waitangi with Key and National MP Jackie Blue, a doctor known to her mother. News reports had stopped referring to Key's 'stunt'. TV ONE's *Close Up* programme interviewed Aroha at Waitangi, and her family in its Auckland studio. The family thought Key's gesture genuine. In Wellington, the government had changed tack, agreeing there was an 'underclass' problem. The *Herald*'s weekly political review considered 'Aroha's big day was of massive assistance to Key's relentless efforts to brand himself as a strong, yet collaborative prime minister-in-waiting' who could 'cross ethnic and socio-economic divides'. 'You cannot buy the kind of publicity National's new leader is getting,' the piece concluded. 'Labour is seething.'

But Key had made himself a hostage to fortune. A year later, Joan Nathan was working part-time for Jackie Blue and said the street had improved. 'There's an alcohol ban down at the reserve. You don't see any of the DMS [youth gang] drinking down there any more. You call the police and they come straight away. We formed a committee and threw a street party in December for the kids.' She said Key checked on them every three or four weeks and Aroha was doing well at school.

Three years later, though, when National was in power, she told TV3's *Campbell Live* the Prime Minister was an 'arsehole' who had done nothing for the poor. 'He's just making everything better for high-earners, not the low-income ones.' She no longer lived in McGehan Close. Aroha, at 16, had been expelled from Mt Albert Grammar and was in Child, Youth and Family care. At last report, 2012, Aroha was working in Australia, earning good money and, at 17, planning to marry.

McGehan Close was clever opposition politics. Key looked not only imaginative and vigorous but genuine and not at all aloof. Reporters' references to the 'rich party leader from Parnell' disappeared from their copy once they had talked to him at McGehan Close. He was, and is, genuine in his impulse to help people. It is an instinct to help them as individuals rather than as a statistical group. Yet McGehan Close was a lesson in the limits of personal assistance. In the end, Key was disappointed. He tells a story of visiting one day and after chatting for a while offering to help tidy up some rubbish. The offer was not well received, unsurprisingly, and he says he went around and picked it up himself.

However, the 'underclass' tack gave him an immediate impact in the polls. A TV3 poll in early February 2007 found him the preferred Prime Minister of 24 per cent, behind Helen Clark's 35 per cent. Key's rating was only one point under the figure Brash had reached after the Orewa speech three years earlier. For TV ONE, Colmar Brunton found six out of 10 believed there was an underclass problem and it had gotten worse under Labour. Key's personal rating in the DigiPoll survey rose from 17 per cent just after becoming National leader to 36 per cent at the end of February.

His next move was quite different – a dealer's move – and it defied conventional political calculations. He made an offer to the Prime Minister that enabled Parliament to outlaw smacking as a method of punishing children. The anti-smacking bill was an issue National could not lose. If the bill passed, it would be seen as one more 'nanny state' intrusion on personal decisions. If it failed, which was looking quite likely, it would be a loss for Helen Clark who strongly supported it. As the bill approached its final reading, Katherine Rich thought she would be the only National MP to vote for it. Paula Bennett wanted to do so but felt 'conflicted' by a rough poll she had run. She had invited 19,000 people to give their opinion and, although only 200 responded, two thirds of them wanted her to oppose the bill. Smacking was a loud issue in public discussion, but as the number who responded to Bennett's survey suggests, the concern did not run deep.

Key had previously proposed an amendment exempting 'minor and inconsequential' smacking, but the bill's sponsor, Green MP Sue Bradford, was prepared to withdraw it rather than pass a law endorsing punitive violence by any definition: the existing law – which did not expressly condone smacking – would be preferable. With the bill in difficulty, Key sent another suggested amendment to Clark. She grabbed it. She wanted the wording slightly altered and Key agreed. The deal was done. They appeared at a press conference together to make the announcement. The amendment in the name of Peter Dunne stated police had discretion not to prosecute 'inconsequential' acts. With its inclusion, the bill passed by 117 votes to three. Only ACT MPs Rodney Hide and Heather Roy, and Taito Phillip Field, no longer with Labour, voted against it.

Most National MPs were astonished that Key so readily neutralised the smacking issue. It is rare to see an opposition leader simply doing the right thing. While commentators gave Clark most of the credit for the compromise, in opinion polls the public rewarded Key. For the first time since 1999 Helen Clark was no longer the preferred Prime Minister.

For the first time, too, house prices were stalling after a long boom. It would be a few months before sales figures would confirm that the worldwide property bubble had finally burst in the first half of 2007. Five years earlier it had cost less than half the average weekly take-home wage to pay the mortgage on the median house in New Zealand. By 2007 the cost had risen to nearly 80 per cent of the average pay packet. First-home seekers were struggling to compete at auctions with investors and immigrants, many of them surprised that New Zealand did not effectively tax capital gains. Regular interest-rate hikes by the Reserve Bank had been having no effect on the demand for large mortgages on low equity and trading banks eagerly fed the market.

Subprime mortgages in the United States began collapsing in 2007 but the ominous sign for the New Zealand market was a sudden drop in net immigration. The end of New Zealand's property boom had an impact on finance companies that had been borrowing at high interest rates for speculative developments. One after another they began to collapse. House prices remained surprisingly stable as the number of sales dwindled. But with prices no longer climbing, households were not borrowing and spending as freely, and the economy was slowing.

Michael Cullen had the country well cushioned for a recession with low public debt. During the boom he had effectively saved an average of $5 billion a year in budget surpluses, all the while ignoring calls from the National Party for tax cuts and doubtless pressure from within his own party for more social outlays. With the surpluses he had reduced public debt and set up two retirement savings vehicles, one the 'Cullen' fund to help pay the baby boom's national superannuation, the other 'KiwiSaver', a scheme to encourage personal retirement savings with a public 'kick-start' contribution. By 2007, when KiwiSaver took effect, Labour was spending more freely, with extended Working for Families benefits, free pre-school education for 20 hours a week and high doctors' subsidies. The additional costs would send the budget back into deficit when the recession struck in 2008 but that would be National's problem. By late 2007 the Labour Government was staring at defeat a year hence, and its frustration was mounting. In one exchange with Key in Parliament, Cullen lost it. 'Scumbag,' Cullen called across the chamber. 'Rich prick.'

In November 2007, Key marked the first anniversary of his leadership with another attempt to tell the country what he stood for, this time with the launch of a 13-minute DVD. The Howard government in Australia had just been defeated by Kevin Rudd's Labor. 'I think it shows voters are willing to embrace change,' said Key. 'I don't think they are looking for radical change, I think they are looking for a change in emphasis, and they'll certainly get that from us.' Neither he nor anyone knew that within a year a crisis in world finance would change the game for an incoming government.

CHAPTER ELEVEN

Road to Victory

John Key gathers all his family around for an election. Liz and Roger, their daughter Milly, Sue and Malcolm and Sue's sons Tim and Riley, had all come up from Christchurch to join John and Bronagh, Stephie and Max, at the big house in Parnell. The night before an election, when the next morning's newspapers cannot by law carry any more campaign argument and the party leaders have made their final pitch for the evening television bulletins, the contenders can do nothing but wait and try to relax for the next 24 hours.

In the sitting room at St Stephens Avenue the night before the 2008 election, Sue Lazar pulled her brother aside for a quiet word. Her younger son, Riley, was voting for the first time and she knew he was feeling obliged to vote National. 'Could you have a chat to him?' she asked.

'Sure,' Key replied, 'no problem.'

Later that night he went to Riley, put a hand on his nephew's shoulder and said, 'Look mate, I want you to know that you can vote for anyone you like tomorrow.' Then, leaning a little closer, he said, 'But just imagine how you'll feel if I lose by one vote.'

It had been a strange campaign, running at the same time as the climax of another election campaign that New Zealand, like the rest of the world, was watching avidly. A young man with the gift of soaring oratory was about to become the first black President of the United States. The New Zealand election was quiet by comparison. Key was no orator. He was much better off the cuff. Earlier in the year, his speechwriters had started to put space in their drafts for him to ad lib. The last gifted orator to lead a New Zealand party had been David Lange, and even then public meetings had ceased to be a feature of election campaigns. The main arena was now the television debate where Labour had thought Helen Clark would have the better of Key.

Though National had been 10 to 15 points ahead in the polls for the best part of three years, Clark had been holding up in the preferred Prime Minister ratings. Labour counted on Key looking loose and unreliable beside her authority and command of fact. The government had thrown him off balance once that year when it found he had owned 100,000 shares in the former rail company Tranz Rail – significantly more than the 40,000 he had said he owned. Key can be careless with factual detail and he had not handled that one well on television. But when it came to the campaign he was on his game.

Broadcaster and Labour Party adviser Brian Edwards has written on his website about the moment in the first television debate that he realised they had underestimated John Key. The leaders were thrown a cute question: 'What does it mean to be rich?' It was put to Clark first.

Mindful no doubt of Michael Cullen's unfortunate 'rich prick' comment the previous year, Clark delivered a fair and reasonable but dull dissertation on how all wealth was relative. When the question was put to Key he said it meant you did not have to work. That was it. He had said it all. Not only did his answer resonate exactly with most people's idea of wealth, it subtly reminded voters that he did not need to be doing this.

It was also a mark of the self-assurance genuine leaders possess. Many party leaders in Key's position would have gladly accepted the opportunity the Prime Minister was giving him to put his personal wealth out of contention in the campaign. A lesser leader would have readily agreed all wealth was relative and his good fortune really did not matter. Yet an answer in those terms would not have rung true and would have sounded defensive. Key simply acknowledged his wealth, as he has always done, without false modesty or the slightest air of superiority. He would also have calculated that most voters were like the woman in Greenhithe when his wealth was highlighted in his first Helensville campaign. For every New Zealander who might envy or resent him, there were probably more who admired it.

There was something of a phony war about the 2008 election campaign, as there was in the US presidential election by that stage, because whoever would be elected knew their policies and plans had already been overwhelmed by a global financial crisis. The poison of subprime mortgage lending in the US had been blended into so many obscure new debt products that when the property bubble burst so did confidence in the US banking system. Early in the year, one investment bank, Bear Stearns, had been bailed out by the US Federal Reserve, but the Fed's chairman, Ben Bernanke, warned in September that further rescues could not be assumed. By then, Americans suffering subprime mortgage foreclosures were reading that Bear Stearns' well-paid traders had completed their gardening leave and were being re-employed in the financial sector. On 13 September one of Wall Street's big five investment houses, Lehman Brothers, was on the brink of collapse. Over that weekend, no buyers could be found and the US government declined to come to its rescue. The collapse sent the American banking system into shock and a seizure went through the financial systems of European countries too.

By the time Lehman Brothers crashed, John Key's old firm, Merrill Lynch, was also in trouble. It was saved by a sale to the Bank of America. Michael Cullen was quick to capitalise. Key, he said, was 'a gambler and short-term money market player who will risk billions of dollars. We are seeing in the United States the consequences of that sort of mentality unfolding right now.' The next day Cullen had another shot. Key did not look as impressive now, he said. 'He's got a short-term profit-maximising mentality, and that is what has brought Merrill Lynch and Lehman Brothers and these other businesses to their knees.' Key called Cullen's comments 'desperate, absurd and pitiful'.

A month later, National and Labour opened their election campaigns on the same Sunday afternoon in Auckland. Though New Zealand's Australian-owned banks had not been infected by the financial 'contagion', the cloud looming over the world economy had become too serious for political points-scoring. Helen Clark launched Labour's campaign in the Town Hall with an announcement that the

ABOVE LEFT: Key, 31, an Auckland currency trader, with his mother Ruth on her 70th birthday, November 1992. FAMILY COLLECTION

ABOVE RIGHT: Enjoying London. John and Bronagh in the city where he led foreign exchange trading for Merrill Lynch from 1996 until 2000. FAMILY COLLECTION

LEFT: Home for a holiday. John with daughter Stephie and son Max at Omaha Beach, north of Auckland. FAMILY COLLECTION

TOP: National's new leader visits McGehan Close in Auckland after highlighting its social problems, 3 February 2007. *HERALD ON SUNDAY*

BOTTOM: Acknowledging applause at the National Party's conference in Wellington, 14 August 2011. *NEW ZEALAND HERALD*

Cycling for tourism, Key crosses a suspension bridge in the Arrow Gorge at the opening of the Queenstown Trail, October 2012. PRIME MINISTER'S STAFF COLLECTION

TOP: High drinks. Celebrating Bronagh's 50th birthday on the flight home from a Commonwealth Heads of Government Meeting in Sri Lanka, November 2013. PRIME MINISTER'S STAFF COLLECTION

BOTTOM: Palace guests. Stephie, Bronagh, John and Max at Balmoral Castle for a weekend with the royal family, September 2013. PRIME MINISTER'S STAFF COLLECTION

government would guarantee bank deposits as Australia had just done. Not far away, at the SkyCity Convention Centre, National Party members heard a Labour-bashing speech from Bill English before a milder address from John Key. He produced a Labour-style pledge card of policy statements and this time did not downplay his financial career. 'I've actually worked in the world of finance and business. Helen Clark hasn't. I've actually picked up a struggling business and made it grow. Helen Clark never has.' Behind the scenes, Key and English as well as Clark and Cullen were receiving regular briefings on the crisis from the Reserve Bank.

When the country is ready to change the government, politicians on both sides are usually the first to know it. They can tell as soon as they go out to engage voters in the streets and shopping malls and supermarkets. If the mood is with them, the eyes of strangers will settle easily on them and many will readily shake their hand. If they are in a government whose time is up, eyes will be averted, and people will edge away to watch them from a distance. Helen Clark slipped and fell during a walkabout in a Christchurch shopping mall, symbolising a campaign in which nothing worked for Labour. Party president Mike Williams made a hurried trip to Melbourne on a word that John Key's signature was on an 'H-fee' document from 20 years before. The signature turned out to be someone else's.

Key, meanwhile, was smiling and hand-shaking his way about the country. *Herald* feature writer Geoff Cumming watched him in Queenstown.

> He's relaxed and upbeat . . . despite the southerly gale blowing off Lake Wakatipu. Locals step forward to shake his hand and wish him luck. Some want his

autograph. People he approaches are mostly foreign tourists, bemused by the television cameras and trailing media but happy to chat. He does small talk well.

However, Cumming noticed that his chatty habit could be a liability when he faced the press.

> Labour has tried to depict Key as unreliable, flip-flopping on issues, changing his story to suit the audience. And he is prone to saying more than he should, then pulling himself up, adding a rider with a schoolboyish grimace. The political hacks know this and ask six variations on the same question.

Under Key, National had 'flip-flopped' on many issues. When the country wants a change of government it generally wants little more than a change of faces, a fresh tone to public discussion, some new policies and priorities. It is not usually looking for a wholesale reversal of the direction the previous government has taken or the dismantling of major programmes it has established. National under Key had dropped its opposition to KiwiSaver, Working for Families income supplements, interest-free student loans, the 'Cullen Fund' for superannuation, Kiwibank, KiwiRail and nuclear-free New Zealand. All of these, of course, National had trenchantly opposed when they were put through Parliament. Then it was an opposition; now it was an incoming government. To counter any fear that he intended to resurrect unfinished business from National's previous time in office, Key had sworn to resign before he would tamper with the terms of New Zealand superannuation in a way that disadvantaged pensioners, and promised that no state assets would be sold or partially sold in his first term.

Winning an election is not just a matter of motivating your sort of people to vote, it also means giving the other side's voters no particular motivation. Michelle Boag has a frank explanation for National's endorsement of Labour programmes such as the waiver of interest on student loans. 'I think his calls on national superannuation, Working for Families, interest-free student loans, were precisely calculated to get him over the line. He knew, and I've heard him say this, that if he said interest-free loans would go, all the students would get out of bed and vote.'

When Key told his nephew on election eve that he could lose by one vote, he was not talking entirely in jest. New Zealand's electoral system gives no guarantee that a party winning more votes than any other by a large margin, but with less than 50 per cent of the count, can form the next government. The fact that the winning party has governed after every election under proportional representation so far has been due to pivotal independent parties led by Peter Dunne and Winston Peters. Subconsciously perhaps, they have held to the Westminster tradition that the party with the largest vote is the rightful government. The one truly daring decision John Key had made before the 2008 election was to rule out a post-election deal with Peters.

Peters had already lost his Tauranga seat in 2005 and his party was polling under the 5 per cent threshold for proportional representation when Key declared he would not, under any circumstances, have him in a National-led government. Even so, it was a courageous call. Peters has a loyal core of admirers who like his ornery, mischievous ways, and he has usually been able to clear the threshold with an election-year outburst on immigration or race relations.

By ruling him out of a National coalition, Key cut off Peters' main source of oxygen in an election campaign: the attention he could attract by keeping the media uncertain which side he might support after the votes were counted. So far, he has never put a second-placed party into power.

On election day 2008, all the Keys of voting age went together to the Parnell District School in St Stephens Avenue where ACT's Rodney Hide that day received 1247 votes to just 311 for National's Richard Worth. The booth returned the heaviest vote for Hide in the electorate he had to win to keep ACT in Parliament as an ally National would probably need.

No matter how predictable the result, election night on television is riveting in every politically interested household. After the polls close at 7 p.m. and the results start coming in around an hour later, the pitiless swing of the pendulum is quickly apparent. Smiling new faces come on screen; familiar ones disappear in defeat. There were cheers in National gatherings as Nikki Kaye took Auckland Central from Judith Tizard, Pansy Wong won the new seat of Botany, and Hamilton West went to National. Louise Upston took Taupo, Todd McClay won Rotorua and John Key held Helensville by the country's largest majority. In Tauranga, youthful Simon Bridges beat Winston Peters by a whopping 10,700, far exceeding Bob 'the builder' Clarkson's 730-vote margin at the previous election.

But the electorate results are not the most important factor any more. Television's moving bar graphs of nation-wide party votes indicate the possible composition of the next government. As the party votes came in, National had 45 per cent, which would give it 58 seats, three short of a majority. Hide's win in Epsom would give ACT five seats for its 3.6 per cent of the vote nationwide. Peters' party, New Zealand First, had 4 per cent, more than ACT but not enough to qualify for list seats. In fact, it succeeded only in taking 4 per cent of the vote out of the count, thereby increasing the proportional allocation of seats to all qualifying parties, including ACT. Key's gamble in ruling Peters out had worked a treat.

Helen Clark conceded in a gracious speech late that night, announcing also her intention to step down from the party leadership. The new Prime Minister-elect was driven with Bronagh to SkyCity where they were greeted with cheers from about 1000 National Party supporters who had been partying as the results came in. The first thing reporters noticed was that Key was now tightly surrounded with security. Locking arms, at least eight police in suits formed a circle around the couple as they made their way from the car. Using their shoulders 'like rugby players', according to one report, the escort pushed a path through party supporters and scrambling media, ignoring the well-wishers' attempts to congratulate Key and oblivious to the blue-and-white streamers raining down.

When he and Bronagh made it to the stage, they were joined by Stephie (15) and Max (13). 'I've got a bit of bad news though, guys,' he told them. 'There's no puppy coming.' It was a reference to Barack Obama's promised reward for his two children in his presidential victory speech four days earlier. The crowd howled in mock outrage. 'Maybe we better reconsider the puppy,' he jested. 'The cat won't like it but we can work our way through that.'

He was 47 years old. He had risen from new MP to Prime

Minister in just six years. Helen Clark had been 18 years in Parliament before she made it to the top. Jim Bolger had also taken 18 years; Sir Robert Muldoon and Norman Kirk, both 15 years. Sir Keith Holyoake had been in and out of Parliament for 28 years altogether. Among politicians who have led a party to election victory in our lifetime, only David Lange's seven years, from a 1977 by-election to the 1984 snap election, can compete with the speed of Key's achievement.

When Key left the party celebration and returned to St Stephens Avenue around midnight, there was a surprise waiting for him. His sisters, Liz and Sue, had decided to mark his triumph with something special. They knew better than anyone how he had dreamed of this night since he was a boy, and how far he had come from those hard early years in Christchurch. Deciding to buy him a piece of pounamu (greenstone), sacred to the South Island iwi Ngai Tahu, they were offered a selection of sculpted items and settled on a large piece representing Aoraki/ Mt Cook. As the highest point in New Zealand, Mt Cook seemed appropriate. Their little brother had scaled the peak of New Zealand politics.

In accordance with Ngai Tahu instructions, all of those giving the pounamu had to be present for its blessing in the sea. So, early on election night, Sue and Liz and their families had slipped away from the Key house to Okahu Bay not far away and performed the rite. The piece has a special place in the Prime Minister's Beehive office today.

CHAPTER TWELVE

Inside the Beehive

O n election night 2008, when the result was becoming clear, calls went out from John Key and his chief of staff Wayne Eagleson to Rodney Hide, Peter Dunne and the Maori Party. By the end of that night, Key and Eagleson had the makings of a government. National had a majority with the support of ACT, but Key wanted a broader government and he wanted it quickly. With the world in the grip of a financial crisis and its leading governments trying to avert a repeat of the 1930s Depression, he was determined to go to an APEC meeting in Peru within two weeks of the election. He wanted the government formed before he left, even if he would not be able to move into the office on the ninth floor of the Beehive until he got back.

Eagleson, previously a private secretary and adviser to Prime Minister Jim Bolger and Don Brash's chief of staff before Key, normally keeps the low public profile of any political leader's right-hand man. But he spoke candidly for this book.

> When you put a deadline on a negotiation you give power to the other guy. ACT was the most difficult. Rodney was wanting the kitchen sink. He had [Business Roundtable's] Roger Kerr in the background continually throwing in new things, but we got there.

It gave National leverage, that the Maori Party had as many seats as ACT.

> We knew that the Maori Party, because of their cultural propensity to talk, would have to hold hui. We said to them, 'We suggest you do it over the next two weeks.' So they went out and organised the hui incredibly quickly. John pushed quite hard. But to be fair, even Rodney never used the time, never tried to play the clock out. He negotiated in good faith and we got there.

Agreements were announced with ACT, the Maori Party and Peter Dunne's United Future eight days after the election, compared to the 32 days it had taken Helen Clark to conclude deals with Dunne and Winston Peters after the previous election. Cabinet positions were announced the next day and all ministers were sworn in bar two, designated foreign minister Murray McCully and trade minister Tim Groser who had left for APEC sessions in advance of the leaders' meetings. Key followed them a few days later, after accepting an offer from Helen Clark for a briefing on the leaders he would meet and how to handle the meetings. They were on the phone for 45 minutes.

While Key was away, the gears of government made a smooth transition thanks mainly to the outgoing Prime Minister. 'Helen Clark was fantastic,' says Eagleson.

> The day after the election, [her chief of staff] Heather
> Simpson called me and said, 'Helen wants me to tell
> you guys that all those constitutional niceties about
> when you can talk to public servants – forget them. I'll
> get Maarten Wevers [head of the Department of the
> Prime Minister and Cabinet] to ring you and you can
> get on with it.'

When Wevers came over to see Eagleson, still in the
opposition wing of the old Parliament Building, he had
a folder that his department had compiled of National's
policies and the legislation that would be needed to fulfil
promises it had made for its first 100 days in office.

The '100-day programme' was not a drastic one. Key
would later be criticised for failing to take the opportunity
presented by the global financial crisis to resume economic
reform. Facing a 'decade of deficits', he could certainly
have convinced the country it could not afford some of
the previous government's obvious profligacy, such as the
interest-free student loans that were generally recognised
to be an extravagant vote-catcher at the 2005 election, and
child benefits for large families on high incomes who did
not need them.

But while crisis response had worked for the fourth
Labour government, it had nearly denied Jim Bolger's
National government a second term. 'One of the things he
was really determined to do from the start,' says Eagleson,
'was to avoid Bolger's mistakes.'

> He and Bolger used to talk about this. I had lived
> through some of those mistakes. We said we would
> get rid of the superannuation surtax and we increased
> it, which probably was the right policy, but John was

determined to be a Prime Minister that kept his
promises. He wanted to incrementally take people with
him rather than do big-bang stuff. He worked on the
theory that New Zealand, even under MMP, doesn't
have a tradition of one-term governments. He took the
view that if we could keep the trust of the public, take
people with us, we could make some changes and be
able to do things.

In Lima, the APEC leaders' meeting concluded with a
communiqué that embarrassed most of them. It declared
they were 'convinced' the global financial crisis would be
over in 18 months. An aide to the outgoing US President
George W. Bush let it be known the clause had been inserted
by the host, Peru's president Alan García. Diplomatically,
Key called it an 'aspirational goal'. He said the leaders were
unanimous that expansionary public spending was needed
even if it meant budget deficits. 'We can get through this
thing. In a large part it is no longer a financial crisis, it is a
crisis of confidence, and people won't invest for the future if
they don't believe we are mapping a pathway to the future.'

Key had met President Bush and China's Hu Jintao and
was particularly impressed by Singapore's Prime Minister
Lee Hsien Loong. Making no effort to hide the thrill of his
first taste of the international stage, he told the *Herald*'s
Audrey Young, 'There is no getting away from the fact
this is a pretty unique experience . . . every so often you
are wandering in and you are thinking not too many New
Zealanders would get to experience this.' Then, reminding
himself that politics is domestic, 'They are the people that
put you there and I think if you lose touch with them they
are the people that take you away pretty quick.'

From Lima, he went to London, mainly to meet Prime

Minister Gordon Brown who had become an authoritative voice in Europe's handling of the financial crisis and had just attended a G20 summit. While there, he also met the Queen, London's entertaining mayor Boris Johnson and the All Blacks on their usual November tour, taking part in a promotion in the giant rugby ball for the 2011 World Cup. In the middle of it all he made the acquaintance of a blood brother he knew nothing about until the *Herald*'s Eugene Bingham researched Key's life for a profile published that year. Bingham tracked down one of the sons of George Key's first marriage.

Older than John by 20 years, Martyn Key came with his wife and son to a London hotel where the half-brothers had a private conversation. He looked 'a bit like my dad', John told reporters later. The older man had been following the New Zealand election and said, 'He is very charismatic. This is all absolutely surreal. I'm stunned but very proud.' They kept in touch. At the time of writing, John said Martyn was gravely ill.

———————

It was December by the time the new Prime Minister returned to hold his first Monday cabinet meeting. He had settled into his new office, or at least found it, which is not always easy in Parliament's distinctive executive wing, the Beehive. As attractive as it is on Wellington's landscape, the interior of the circular building is disorienting. Offices occupy the outer ring of each floor with the lifts and foyers in a central core. The foyers are identical, as are the entrances to the ministers' suites, except for the ninth floor where a staffed bureau guards double doors into the Prime Minister's office.

Inside that office, John Key's desk occupies one end of the room facing a setting of sofas around a low table. The view out the window to his left is stunning. All the rooms have spectacular outlooks, over Wellington Harbour or Parliament grounds or the city to the south, but since they are segmented views and there is a full circle of them, they give a newcomer no sense of direction.

Key works at his desk with his back to enlarged and framed front pages of the *Herald on Sunday* and the *Sunday Star-Times* trumpeting his 2008 election victory. The wall to his right bears framed photographs of his children and his visits with distinguished figures. Framed on the far wall is a black athletics singlet with a silver fern worn by Peter Snell at an Olympic Games. Alongside it, facing Key at his desk, there is an oil painting composed of a collage of Helensville images. It is the work of Auckland painter Nicky Foreman, who has also done a splendid mural for a stairway of the Parnell residence.

A personal assistant works in an adjoining office behind him. In front of him a door leads to a 'back office' with a large meeting table and walls decorated with framed All Blacks jerseys that he has bought at charity auctions. One of them is signed by Stan Meads, brother and locking partner of the great Colin Meads in the 1960s. Beyond the back office is a small bathroom for the Prime Minister's use. The next room is Eagleson's office. A narrow corridor from Eagleson's room makes a circuit of the rest of the floor, passing the rooms of speechwriters, press secretaries, a diary secretary, a staff meeting room and advisers' offices. Most of them had moved across from the old building on the weekend before Key returned from London.

That Monday, Key began the schedule he would follow almost every week he is in the country. He wakes in Auckland in time for a 6 a.m. call from Newstalk ZB to record the first of his weekly chats, now done with numerous radio stations on Monday mornings. Then he heads to TVNZ for a weekly appearance on its *Breakfast* programme. He catches the 8.35 flight to Wellington, greeting many of the fellow passengers going to the capital on business for the day. Reaching his office around 10 a.m., he receives a briefing from officials on issues he will face in the cabinet meeting, then sits down in his office with a 'kitchen cabinet' of Bill English, Gerry Brownlee, Steven Joyce and Murray McCully.

The full cabinet is waiting on the floor above, in a windowless room occupying the whole top floor of the Beehive. Ministers sit in ranked order around a large doughnut of connected desks. The artificial lighting is bright and the acoustics enable a comment made anywhere in the room to be heard by everyone present. Key chairs the meeting and often has to arbitrate on disagreements, particularly between the economic and environmental teams. 'I have to make the call. In the end if I say, "No, we're doing this", they go "Okay".' The cabinet may go well into the afternoon and at some point there will be a formal meeting with the Governor-General, constituted as the Executive Council, for legislation and regulations to be formally signed into law.

Around 4 p.m. the Prime Minister goes down to a small theatre on the ground floor of the Beehive where the press gallery and television cameras are waiting for the post-cabinet news conference. Before he goes in there, he meets his press secretaries, experienced former news gatherers themselves, who brief him on the questions they think he is likely to be asked. No matter how perceptive, however, they will not have anticipated many of the questions, often prickly and sometimes desultory, that may come from the 40 or more reporters, commentators and correspondents in the room. The Monday press conference is a news feast. Any view the Prime Minister expresses on a subject is likely to be of interest simply because it carries the power of his position. The questions come hard and fast, each reporter seizing the chance when they get one. The angles they take on an issue, the spin they are going to give it for a story, can be wildly unpredictable. Prime Ministers have to be quick on their feet.

John Key, that first day, fielded questions ranging from an emergency in Bangkok – where violent political demonstrations had closed the airport and 200 New Zealanders were among 230,000 tourists unable to get out – to National's plans for reversing Labour's phase-out of incandescent light bulbs. Key hoped people could get out of Bangkok on Thai Airways flights from a military airport. The cabinet had discussed other options but he would not go into details. A few questions later he said one of the options was to send an Air Force 747 or charter an Air New Zealand flight. After the press conference, it turned out that both the RNZAF's Boeings were under maintenance in the United States. Labour's likely new leader, Phil Goff, the previous government's Minister of Defence, went on the offensive, asking why Key had not contacted Australian Prime Minister Kevin Rudd for a co-ordinated response. He suggested Key ask him or Helen Clark for advice on handling a crisis. It was not a great start.

With the press conference over, Key goes back up to his office, or joins one or two cabinet committee meetings that get under way about 5 p.m. At 6 he breaks for 10 minutes to watch the first few items on the evening television news. That night the stranded Kiwis in Bangkok and his press conference response lead on both channels. Then he grabs something to eat. There are dining rooms for ministers and MPs on the Beehive's lower floors but Key prefers to cook something in his electric frying pan in the ninth-floor kitchen. He and Eagleson keep a 'reasonably generous source of whitebait' there for quick meals. (Eagleson, he says, makes a great fritter.) From 8 p.m. they have scheduled meetings in his office with delegations from interest groups or one of the government's partner parties with an issue that needs a quiet discussion. Around 10 p.m., visitors leave, Key and Eagleson go into their respective offices, close the door and attack the piles of paper on their desks.

Stacks of paper follow a Prime Minister everywhere he goes. It travels in thick black briefcases, a new one delivered to him every day. Inside there are papers for the next cabinet meeting containing policy analysis and options, advice from different departments and summary notes on top. Each paper has a 'cabinet top' and a 'pag' note (from the policy advisory group in the Department of the Prime Minister and Cabinet). Besides cabinet papers, the briefcase on a typical day brings Treasury reports on economic data, international and domestic, especially on the US and Australian economies, and analyses of the data. Other folders contain staff reports on subjects in the news he needs to know more about, advice on what individual ministers are about to do, management reviews of ministers, updates on their priorities, papers on subjects he is taking a particular interest in, papers for his own portfolio, tourism. The foreign ministry sends him reports every day. He approves ministerial travel requests, or not. There are 'traffic light' messages telling him of progress in certain projects, draft answers for oral questions in Parliament. Reading it all takes him several hours a day.

'I love plane trips – nobody can ring me up and interrupt me – though I don't read cabinet papers on a plane. Too risky.'

It is not uncommon for Beehive lights to be on well after midnight. The hours worked by Bill Birch, Minister of Finance in the Bolger government, are legendary. There is a story – Eagleson insists it's true – that Birch once scheduled a meeting for 12 o'clock and when the officials turned up at midday they were told the minister meant midnight. Key used to work past midnight until people told him he was looking tired. Nowadays he stops about 11.30 p.m. and gets driven up the hill to Premier House in Tinakori Road. There, after wishing the duty policeman goodnight, he climbs the stairs to the far-from-salubrious apartment for prime ministers on the second floor.

He normally sleeps in Premier House on Tuesday and Wednesday nights too, especially when Parliament is in session. Bronagh and the family have not moved to Wellington. It is not that she doesn't like the capital, she explains. 'I actually really like Wellington. We had three years there in the eighties and it wasn't my idea of where I wanted to be – we'd left Christchurch for the big OE, got to Melbourne and John got the job back in Wellington – but I really enjoyed it.' When they returned from overseas the Parnell house was under construction, and by the time her husband won the keys to Premier House, Stephie and Max were at high school. 'They were both settled and they'd had lots of changes, so we decided to stay in Auckland. It worked well because when John's down there he doesn't have to worry about us.' He does, of course. He calls frequently.

Peter Dunne, Revenue Minister in the government, was with Key in the Beehive one morning when news broke of a tragedy involving a pupil at King's, the private school Max attended. The news item said the school was sending pupils home. Key was unable to reach Bronagh to ensure she'd heard and would be there when Max arrived, so phoned places in Auckland where he thought she might be. At each place, he got someone on the phone who didn't believe him when he said, 'Hello, it's John Key here, I'm trying to reach . . .' Dunne watched him try several places with the same result and marvelled that Key didn't explode.

> Here was a man genuinely concerned for his son, having to put up with this. I felt for him – if I'd been in his position I'd have screamed at someone. That is the sort of guy he is. He didn't want somebody else to ring Bronagh, he wanted to do it himself. That family link is pretty important to him.

Key wakes in the apartment about 5.30 on Tuesday and Wednesday mornings and usually goes for a jog with his police escort, up to Karori Road and back down the hill to Parliament. Warmed up, the workout continues in the Beehive gym, often with some boxing. He is allowed to hit the cops but they are not supposed to hit back. 'One of them has clocked me – it was quite amusing.'

Thursday mornings are different. Though Parliament is still sitting, prime ministers take that day and the next for engagements around the country. With any luck, he will be at home in Auckland that night. His weekend is less busy but he does not put aside a particular part of it for leisure. If he can schedule Saturday appointments in the morning he can watch Max play rugby in the afternoon. He gets to about half the games. Saturday evening may be free, but just as often there is a function to attend. Sunday is quieter. If Max is free they will play golf at some stage; if he is not,

Key will go to a driving range. He intends to play much more golf one day. Sunday brings no respite from cabinet papers. Reading for the next day's meeting will take two or three hours of Sunday plus calls to ministers if there is something coming from them that gives him concern. Sunday night he often calls Bill English or Steven Joyce to prepare for Monday morning's media calls.

That is the week ahead of him when he wakes in Premier House on a Tuesday morning. Tuesday has cabinet committee meetings in the morning – and cabinet committees in John Key's government are more interesting than most, for Key, unlike his predecessor, has invited ministers from supporting parties to stay in the room.

CHAPTER THIRTEEN

Partners in Power

Less than five years since a National Party leader had
denied Maori deserved any special recognition in
New Zealand as tangata whenua, original people
of the land, a new National leader brought an independent
Maori party into his government. John Key's partnership
with the Maori Party, for at least the first six years of his
tenure, could turn out to be his most important legacy
for New Zealand. Going into the 2014 election the
Maori Party was no longer figuring in his post-election
calculations, but not because National voters disliked the
deal. Quite the opposite. Since the Brash outburst 10 years
earlier, Key had broadly reconciled conservative voters
to the Maori case for respectful consultation, if not extra
rights, in the government of the country. The problem for
the Maori Party was that its partnership with National
had not materially improved the condition of its people.
Founding co-leaders Tariana Turia and Pita Sharples were
retiring at the election and the party's prospects of survival

looked slim. But if all, or almost all, the Maori electorates return to the Labour Party in time, it seems unthinkable that their representatives will not enjoy a more distinct and influential role than in previous Labour governments. If they do, they will have Tariana Turia, Pita Sharples and John Key to thank for it.

Typically, Key explains his embrace of the Maori Party in down-to-earth political terms rather than its historic possibilities.

> I dallied with the idea before the [2008] election but we didn't really talk about it. After the election I thought the margins were really tight and what looked like a rock-solid majority [with ACT's five MPs and Peter Dunne] could change. Also, I thought they would add more balance to the government. I just thought, 'I reckon they are good people and we will be a better government if we listen to them.' Most people want us to solve race relations issues, they want us to deal with Treaty claims and they want us to get a harmonious society. And I actually truly believe New Zealand is bicultural. It's a multicultural country with a bicultural foundation. I think it understands that, but every so often when people think it has been pushed too far, there is the Don Brash response.

When Key announced his government, Turia and Sharples were named as ministers outside the cabinet, as were ACT's Rodney Hide and Heather Roy, and Peter Dunne. New Zealand has had six elections using mixed member proportional representation (MMP) and, contrary to expectations, the country is not developing a tradition of coalition government where ministers of more than one party comprise the supreme decision-making body, the cabinet. The first attempted coalitions, National with New Zealand First in 1996 and Labour with the Alliance in 1999, did not end happily. Thereafter, both National and Labour have found it more practical to be minority governments with the support of smaller parties that also prefer to keep their distance from the dominant party. Rather than full coalitions, the usual arrangement has become 'confidence and supply' agreements that bind the smaller partner to vote with the larger party in Parliament only on issues of confidence in the government and (financial) supply. On all other issues, the smaller party, including its ministers, remains free to vote against government bills it does not like.

The Maori Party's negotiated agreement with National contained few specific policies but plenty of hopeful principles for dealing with each other. Turia told Audrey Young her party had entered the negotiations with one purpose in mind, 'that if we were able to achieve a respectful relationship, a mana-enhancing relationship, then anything was possible'. One of the few specific elements of the agreement was that the government would not pursue National's long-standing policy to abolish the separate Maori seats, and the Maori Party would not press its aim to have the seats 'entrenched' in the Electoral Act, which would mean they could not be abolished by a bare majority of Parliament.

National's other principal partner, ACT, with as many seats as the Maori Party (five), had negotiated a more detailed agreement. ACT secured a taskforce reviewing government spending, a productivity commission, a parliamentary review of Labour's carbon emissions trading scheme and a '2025 Taskforce' headed by Don Brash to look at the economy that far ahead. ACT had brought Sir Roger Douglas back to Parliament on its list and also hoped he would be made a minister. Key quickly made it clear he would not have him. Nor was he much interested in Brash's taskforce. When it produced its first report at the end of 2009 – recommending, among other things, that $9 billion be slashed from the $40 billion budget and the top tax rate be reduced to 20–25 cents in the dollar – Key and English barely acknowledged it.

Dunne, with only one vote to offer, had not been in a position to negotiate very much. He was largely content to be Minister of Revenue as he had been previously in the Labour-led government. Explaining the technicalities of taxation is not a task that many politicians are anxious to take on.

But the Maori Party's prime interest, its relationship with Key's government, had an immediate consequence for the way the government has functioned with all its partners. Peter Dunne, who has been a minister outside the cabinet of successive Labour and National governments, was surprised when he joined the Key ministry to be told he was welcome to sit in on cabinet committees, where the details of decisions to be made by the cabinet are worked out with the help of official advisers. Departmental officials do not attend full cabinet meetings as a rule. Helen Clark, according to Dunne, had followed the convention that confidence and supply ministers would be compromised if they were on the committees.

> With Clark you came to a cabinet committee when something within your portfolio or your support agreement was up for discussion. After that you were kicked out, which I thought was correct at

the time because you were not tainted by the rest of the decisions. You could say, 'I wasn't party to that discussion, wasn't there.'

When Dunne told Key about this arrangement, Key's view was, 'That's silly. If you want to attend cabinet committees you can. Basically it's your decision. You decide how involved you want to be.' It was made clear to Dunne and the others that not only could they take part in all committee discussions but they were under no obligation to support any decision made there if they disagreed with it. Key imposed only one condition: they must never reveal what is said in the committees.

Eagleson confirms the arrangement and says it started with the Maori Party.

> When we came in, the Maori Party were keen to try to influence everything, so we said, we'll invite you to these cabinet committees and accept that there are some things that go on there that you guys will go and vote against in Parliament. The one requirement – the absolute requirement – we gave them was confidentiality, and they have always honoured that.

Initially, he says, Rodney Hide declined the offer. ACT did not want its position possibly compromised on decisions it might not like and did not want its ministers bound by confidentiality about what might be discussed. Dunne had qualms too. 'I found it a wee bit strange in terms of the traditional concept of collective cabinet responsibility.' But like Turia and Sharples, Dunne took it up, and eventually the ACT ministers did too. According to Eagleson, 'We said to them, look, we are giving you the opportunity to influence government, raise points and have your cake and eat it too by being able to walk out of the room and vote against something. You'd be nuts not to take this up.'

But there are times when it is better not to receive information in circumstances where you cannot repeat it. 'On a couple of occasions,' says Dunne, 'I didn't feel comfortable getting the level of knowledge I was when I was not going to be supporting the decision, so I didn't go to those meetings.' One of the instances occurred early in the life of the government when National was repealing a business tax credit for research and development that Dunne had implemented for the previous government. He says it is completely up to the support ministers to decide how engaged they want to be.

> It is an evolution. The idea of confidence and supply ministers was an innovation of Helen Clark. She was trying to protect the partners from being swamped as they had been in the previous coalitions. It worked to an extent but you ended up being out of the loop on a lot of things and looking a bit silly sometimes. People would say, 'You're a minister in this government, don't you know what it's doing?' Clark was putting a fence around you to protect you, [whereas] Key's view was, you protect yourself, it's your job on the line. I think it's better. You determine your own rules. You work better with other ministers too because you are not just popping in for your item, you are there as of right.

The day-to-day management of a government's dealings with other parties falls mostly on the Prime Minister's chief of staff. With 59 seats in a Parliament of 122 after the 2008 election, National needed the support of either ACT or the Maori Party, but not both, to pass any piece of legislation. Eagleson would ensure that any proposed legislation was run past all supporting parties.

> The way it works is that the minister in charge of the bill will have his political adviser approach the Maori Party, United Future and ACT through their political staff and offer them a briefing from officials. The minister might also have a chat to them. We do that with Labour, the Greens and New Zealand First sometimes too because a lot of the bills are relatively non-controversial. The Maori Party get way more briefings than anybody else because they ask for more.
>
> When it looks like the partner parties are not going to vote for something, I will meet their chiefs of staff, usually on a Friday morning, and go through what has happened. I will try to resolve it and often will. Then, every month, John, Bill [English] and I will sit down with each of the support parties and have a catch-up. Obviously, if there are major dramas or crises or disagreements, that is where they will get thrashed out.

Well, not always, he admits. At the time of writing, National could not convince the Maori Party and Dunne to support a Resource Management Act amendment that would give economic development equal consideration with environmental protection. 'So, we have a real issue getting that over the line but no one is yelling and screaming, there's no brow-beating. We are working our way through – who knows where it will end up? We may have to keep it for another day.'

It does not pay the governing party to assume a

partner will support anything without consultation, even legislation that is in line with the smaller party's policies. Eagleson mentions a classic mistake National made.

> It was in our first term. Nick Smith, Minister for ACC, had a sensible bill to liberalise accident insurance with more private-sector involvement. He made the assumption ACT would vote for it because while it didn't go as far as they wanted, it was a move in that direction. The others [Maori Party and Dunne] hated it. Nick went out there and announced we were going to do it. Rodney Hide said, 'Well, you haven't asked me. I haven't given you my vote yet.' At that point there was a negotiation. It's very difficult to have a negotiation when you have said you will do it. So Rodney managed to screw us. He extracted more out of us. Fair enough, we weren't organised. It was a pretty good lesson about having all your ducks in a row before you go out publicly.

Awkward conflicts can also occur when the partners disagree with something National wants to do in a portfolio held by a minister in the smaller party.

> The way confidence and supply has developed is that if a cabinet decision is taken within their portfolio they are bound to vote for it. But we try to narrow the issue down so that, for example, Pita [Sharples], as Associate Minister of Corrections, didn't like something being done in that portfolio and we said you can vote against it. We have loosened the constitutional conventions quite a lot to maintain a collegial kind of government.

Eagleson believes it is working well.

> In the first six months after the 2008 election some of
> the press gallery got worked up over the fact that the
> Maori Party voted against a lot of our legislation. We
> said, 'That's fine, they're supporting us on confidence
> and supply.' Now, the Maori Party vote against us on
> any number of occasions and not one journalist gets
> excited about it.

However, the relationship is not always 'collegial' between
the support parties, particularly ACT and the Maori Party.
ACT invited Tariana Turia to address its 2009 conference,
and she did so, but in August that year an issue in Rodney
Hide's local government portfolio looked capable of
blowing John Key's partners apart. Hide had inherited an
Auckland 'super city' project from the previous government and was proceeding with enthusiasm to unite the
city's six municipalities and its regional council into a
single Auckland Council. In June he went to the Prime
Minister and offered to give up the portfolio because he
could not put his name on a bill that would reserve two
seats for Maori on the Auckland Council. Key suggested
the Maori seats be legislated with an amendment that
Hide would not need to introduce. Hide declined the offer,
though he did not make it a public issue. It became public
in August after National MP Tau Henare tried to raise
support in his caucus for the Maori seats on the council.
Tariana Turia declared it 'sad for the country when we
have a politician who continues to play this card every time
there is a significant issue'. Hide prevailed, but he agreed
that instead of two council seats, Maori would have a nine-
member statutory board that would appoint representatives

with voting rights to the council's committees.

The Maori Party had its share of success, though. Early in the term, Key surprisingly agreed to let a flag previously associated with a Maori sovereignty movement fly alongside the New Zealand flag on the Auckland harbour bridge for Waitangi Day. 'Why wouldn't we do that?' Key asks, again with little apparent interest in the historic or symbolic weight of what he was doing. He also agreed to the Maori Party's call for New Zealand to sign the United Nations Declaration of the Rights of Indigenous Peoples. 'When we signed the DRIP all hell broke loose [but] it is non-binding. We had great legal advice that even if we didn't sign it, as Australia and America haven't, it would be recognised in New Zealand law anyway.'

Most important for the Maori Party, its founding issue, the foreshore and seabed, was resolved with legislation that conferred a legal status on the coast that was not significantly different from Labour's, except that a Maori party had helped to formulate the law this time. For the party's Tai Tokerau MP, Hone Harawira, it was the last straw. Never comfortable in a partnership with National, Harawira left the party in 2011 and with the help of former Alliance organiser Matt McCarten and perennial Pakeha protesters John Minto and Sue Bradford, formed the Mana Party to contest the Maori seats.

When John Key invited the Maori Party into the government he hoped they would 'end up taking us out of our comfort zone', and in certain areas, he says, they have. Whanau Ora was one example. Previous governments have been uncomfortable with the idea of entrusting public money to self-help programmes. Looking back on the Maori partnership, Key says, 'I reckon we have been a way better government for it. Tariana has been great. She is principled and sometimes she's moody but she's really good to deal with. She's straightforward.' In this context he also mentions National's Hekia Parata. As Minister of Education, 'she gets a lot of flak but her perspective [on Maori] is more sophisticated than Pita's and Tariana's. Theirs is more grass-roots, [whereas] she's been in Te Puni Kokiri [Ministry of Maori Development] and when you ask her things about Maoridom she will tell you what's myth and what's real.' Maori poverty, he believes, is the reason the Maori Party is struggling to survive.

> I have been to lots and lots of really poor places with Tariana and Pita. Fundamentally, their constituency is really poor and recessions are toughest on those people. You go to Gisborne, Porirua and South Auckland and the recession has been tough on them. [*Herald* columnist] Deborah Hill Cone wrote a column asking if I'd been to Kaikohe recently. The answer is yes, and to places way worse than that. I've been up the East Coast and I've seen it in my own electorate. Some of the marae are really, really poor, but it is private property.

Tribal authority is also real. The ink had barely dried on National's agreement with the Maori Party when Key had a visit from representatives of Nga Puhi, Tainui, Tuwharetoa, Ngati Porou, Whanganui and Ngai Tahu. A few days later he and Dr Sharples, Minister of Maori Affairs, went at the invitation of the Tuwharetoa paramount chief, Tumu Te Heuheu, to a hui at Pukawa marae on the southern shore of Lake Taupo, where he also met Tuku Morgan (Tainui), Sonny Tau (Tai Tokerau), Api Mahuika (Ngati Porou), Mark Solomon (Ngai Tahu), Archie Taiaroa (Whanganui) and Tumanako Wereta (Tuwharetoa). The iwi leaders said they supported National's approach to the Maori Party but made it clear that *they* represented the Treaty partner.

The Maori Party does not challenge the pre-eminence of the iwi leaders' forums. In fact, Te Ururoa Flavell, the party's new co-leader, counts it a success that it has been able to open the door to the iwi leaders and give them access to Key and English. 'A case in point was the carbon credits issue [in the emissions trading scheme, affecting the value of forestry on iwi estates]. The iwi leaders' group felt it was a key issue for them. We open the door, go along to support their case and do follow-up afterwards at their request.'

The loose coalitions that now prevail in New Zealand can produce some interesting alliances on legislation. The Maori Party supported ACT's charter schools proposal in the Parliament elected in 2011. Without the Maori Party that legislation would not have passed since Peter Dunne did not support it. Dunne describes 'a developing dynamic among support partners' where 'we can leverage off each other a bit'.

> One supports something another wants to do in return for support on things that matter to it. Take my game industry bill [passed in November 2013]. I didn't want to tell people who cared about that bill that I couldn't get the numbers because I had opposed something they didn't care about.

Key, according to Dunne, would prefer all of them onside for each other.

> Clark was different. She was focused on 61 votes and it didn't matter where they came from. Key tends to say, 'I've got 64 votes and I'll do what I can to maintain 64.'

He would like to keep the team together and he puts a
lot of effort into that.

The partners get invitations to National caucus parties, and
they are invited to nominate people for appointments and
to suggest subjects for inquiry by standing commissions.

That sort of thing didn't happen under Labour because
you were not on the team to the same extent. This is
just the system evolving. When Peters and I went
into coalition with Clark we were styled ministers
outside the government. The styling under Key is
ministers supporting the government. It is a subtle and
significant shift.

CHAPTER FOURTEEN

Popular Joker

A nation seldom gets to know a politician in a major party very well until that person becomes Prime Minister. One reason is that the head of a government naturally attracts more attention than the leader of an opposition because governments can act, while oppositions can seldom do more than talk. But another reason is that modern elections, contested crucially on television, are won by a party leader, and with that public success comes a singular freedom to be the person they are. They may take advice, but ultimately no minister or media adviser is in a position to overrule what a Prime Minister's instincts tell him or her to say and do. John Key's instincts, it quickly became evident, told him to ignore a great deal of conventional advice.

Advice such as never put anything on your head when a camera is around. In fact, never go near anyone or any situation that might give the media an embarrassing photograph or video clip that will be endlessly republished:

clips such as Don Brash teetering as he walked a plank onto a yacht; or Sir Geoffrey Palmer playing his trumpet on the Beehive balcony for the *Holmes* programme because he had been advised it would help to popularise his image. John Key, too, was soon putting himself in situations of considerable publicity risk. In February 2009, three months after the election, he went to Auckland's Big Gay Out festival, which seems an unremarkable gesture now because he has made a habit of attending it since. But in 2009 it was a courageous move for a Prime Minister from a conservative party who had not supported a civil union bill some years before.

Key carried it off, doing his best to dance with two hefty transvestites, Buffy and Bimbo, and receiving a hug from Ivy who told the *Herald* he was really Robert van Dijk, a Labour supporter. That night, when the Keys were watching television and the item with Buffy and Bimbo had played, Max looked sideways at his father and said, 'You do realise I go to a boys' school?' A Prime Minister who surprises his supporters can have an incalculable influence on public opinion. Within four years, the National Party's northern regional conference would endorse adoption by couples of the same sex and National MP Nikki Kaye was working with the Greens' Kevin Hague on a draft bill. Within five years Parliament would pass a bill recognising same-sex marriage after Key gave it early support.

Not that all of his contributions in that area are appreciated. His ribbing of a radio host for wearing a 'gay red top' required some explanation. The word in that context meant 'weird' he said. 'Young people use it all the time. I don't think many people would be offended by it. If someone is, I apologise for it.' That was the same day he told pupils at a Dunedin high school British soccer star David

Beckham was 'thick as bat shit'. He probably has never worn that day's tie or cufflinks again. Key is superstitious about these things. Likewise, Bronagh has no doubt confiscated whatever he was wearing the day he was asked a baited question at a post-cabinet press conference about whether he would send a child to a fully or partially funded early childhood centre, if his wife were to have another baby.

'I'd be extremely worried,' replied Key, 'because I've had a vasectomy.'

The press conference went silent.

He can laugh about it now, but Bronagh adds, 'His wife was not amused.'

Early in his first year of office Key went on American television's *Late Show with David Letterman* at the request of Tourism New Zealand who had paid a public relations firm $10,000 for setting it up. They stood him alone in the middle of the stage. Letterman looked disengaged; the Prime Minister looked like a rube.

'You're near Tasmania – is that correct?' asked Letterman.

'Yeah, and sort of Australia,' responded Key.

'How many years ago did you get on the plane to come here?' Letterman quipped.

'Well, I've aged a lot, yeah.'

'Do you get mail down there?' Letterman continued.

'Oh sure, yeah – by pigeon.'

He also had to read a list of 10 jokey reasons to visit New Zealand. Give him his due, he was game, and Tourism NZ chief executive Kevin Bowler was pleased. 'We got 10 minutes of our Prime Minister talking about New Zealand on prime television watched by millions, plus all the YouTube hits it generated. It was one of the best-value things we've done in the last couple of years.'

Sometimes, however, Key is a little too game. The day a former New Zealand cricket captain, Stephen Fleming, phoned to ask if he would come down to the Basin Reserve during a fundraiser for the Christchurch earthquake appeal and face an over from Shane Warne, Key said, 'Yeah, sure.' Key had not played cricket. His economic adviser, Grant Johnston, had played the game and as soon as he heard, he told Key, 'That's a mistake, get out of it.' Batting looks easy on television. It is not. It is hard enough to hit a ball hurled by any competent bowler, let alone Australia's most celebrated leg spinner.

This time Key heeded the advice, though he did not pull out. Instead, he called Fleming back and requested some coaching.

> Stephen took me down to the nets and we had a couple of hours' practice over a couple of days. On the next Saturday morning, I made some local kids give me a bat. All the kids started coming over to watch and the bowling got quicker. But everything was fine and when we got to the celebrity thing I was sure it was going to be perfect. The place was packed, thousands of people there. Then, just as I was about to go out, Stephen turned around and said, 'Gee, I hope I haven't stuffed this up.' I said, 'That's a great vote of confidence.' He went, 'You should be all right.' I went out there thinking, 'I'm just going to smack it.' But it was fine – Shane Warne was great.

Warne bowled full tosses. Key connected quite well, hitting three balls to the square leg boundary. When he tackles anything, he wants to know how to do it well.

The one video clip Key regrets – though probably he need not – was his catwalk act at the launch of a uniform for Rugby World Cup staff.

> We got there and they put us in this stuff. Paula Bennett had done a catwalk piss-take and everybody was wolf-whistling, laughing and chanting at me to do it. So I just strutted down. It wasn't until afterwards, when I heard a cameraman from TV3 say, 'This is a ripper', that I realised what would happen and thought, 'Oh God, I'm dead meat.'

Incidents such as these play well for Key because they look less like publicity stunts than publicity risks, which they are. In fact, most political commentary still cites the catwalk strut as an error and the clip continues to be aired on television at every opportunity. But it is doubtful that it did him any damage. People can recognise when a man is simply having fun in a way that comes naturally to him. The more ordinary and even error-prone Key appears in these moments, the more it works as a counterpoint to his wealth and business success. Those could easily work against him in politics if he was not seen to be so transparently normal and even average in other respects.

The polls in the first year of government went into the stratosphere for Key personally and National which hit a high of 58 per cent in a TV3 Reid Research Poll in August 2009. By November the party's numbers were returning to more normal levels for a new government but Key's personal ratings were going higher. In his review of the year, John Armstrong called him 'nothing short of a political phenomenon'. Key was 'rewriting the rules of New

Zealand politics . . . National's post-election dream run is overwhelmingly down to Key's strong rapport with voters, especially females who shunned National in the past.' Another *Herald* columnist, Garth George, who normally took a grim view of politicians and all their works, had met the new Prime Minister and was impressed.

> He is amiable, engaging, good-natured, highly intelligent, humorous and, most of all, unaffected. You feel comfortable in his presence; there is no 'side' to him, no insistence on protocol, no efforts to protect him from the hoi polloi. And one of his most attractive traits, which he makes no effort to hide, is his unbridled enthusiasm for, and utter delight in, being Prime Minister.

There is no 'side' to Key in the sense that nothing seems to be hidden. In private and in public, he is open-faced and talkative. Advisers would say he is talkative to a fault in stand-up interviews with reporters. He is usually willing to answer as many questions as they want to ask, no matter how repetitive. His attentive patience can give an issue exaggerated importance, but to close off further questions and walk away always suggests a politician has something to hide. Key's instinct is probably wiser than the advice.

There was, of course, another, less visible, reason for his popularity. He had done nothing in those early years in office to antagonise any group of voters. He had come to power when the country was in recession, the world was in a financial crisis and governments of leading economies were casting fiscal caution to the winds to avoid a rerun of the Great Depression. New Zealand, thanks to its Australian banks, and Australia, thanks to China, were comparatively well off. The previous National and Labour governments had been running budget surpluses for 14 years and public debt was below 10 per cent of the nation's GDP.

The outgoing finance minister, Michael Cullen, had budgeted for a deficit in 2008–09 exactly as economic orthodoxy prescribes to help a country through a recession. But Cullen's previous surpluses were based on tax rates that National had promised to cut and a level of public spending that would be unsustainable at lower tax rates. Labour's spending included at least two notable programmes that were not restricted to the needy: child benefits called 'Working for Families' that extended to large families on high incomes, and interest-free student loans.

Both offered ready savings for an incoming government facing the fiscal consequences of recession, rising welfare needs and falling tax revenue, and receiving Treasury advice that without substantial savings budget deficits would continue for a decade with dire consequences for the country's economic security. In these circumstances, the public might have absolved National of its pre-election commitment to keep both programmes intact, especially as the commitments had been made before Lehman Brothers collapsed, triggering the global financial crisis. But breaking an election commitment in any circumstances was just about the last thing that John Key intended to do. His finance minister, Bill English, a member of the previous National cabinet, was of like mind.

> John had set a tone in opposition that was upbeat, aspirational and moderate. This guy was not going to break the furniture. Lehmans crashed the day after we launched our tax package. We'd made undertakings about no changes to Working for Families, no changes

to national super, no changes to student loans, all prior
to Lehman's crash. John was clear: we were going to
stick to all those undertakings. Any other politician
would have said, 'We've got the opportunity to change
everything we said, put it off the table.' I can still
remember the sheer relief of figuring out this guy had
the confidence to be flexible. I didn't want to relive the
opportunism of the 1990s. You lose credibility. People
know you are being opportunistic. On the face of it, we
had good reason in the 1990s for doing the things we
did, but we survived by one seat [Waitaki] on a recount
three weeks after election night [1993].

In the 2008 recession, English did not believe spending
cuts were immediately necessary. 'We had a big drop
in revenue but we had borrowing capacity. Cullen was
right about that, debt levels were low.' So they deepened
the deficit the next year with a tax cut in April and extra
relief for people made redundant, plus tax arrangements to
help small businesses with cash-flow problems, additional
spending on schools, roads and state houses to stimulate
more economic activity, and money for ideas from a Prime
Minister's 'job summit' in February which included wage
subsidies for a nine-day fortnight and a national cycleway.
The only move they made to reduce the deficit was to put
off the second and third stages of their planned tax cuts
indefinitely.

The economy emerged from its 18-month recession in
the second quarter of 2009 but the recovery was marginal
and another cloud appeared over the global economy in the
shape of Greece. Its public debt was proving unsustainable
for an economy using a currency shared by strong
economies with less profligate government, especially

Germany. It was already apparent Greece would not be the only euro-using country in that predicament. The New Zealand Treasury's December economic and fiscal update warned: 'The impact from the next shock could be larger than after the GFC because the world economy is less well positioned.'

After a year in office, though, it was past time for the government to be considering New Zealand's deeper economic problems – especially the weight of private investment going into residential property rather than productive industries. A Victoria University tax working group was contemplating a serious capital gains tax, common in other countries but long demonised in New Zealand. English drew frequent attention to an Inland Revenue survey of 100 of the country's wealthiest individuals that found only half of them paying the top tax rate. But when the working group reported in January 2010, it found a capital gains tax too complicated, recommending a complex land tax instead. The government rejected that too, settling for a removal of housing depreciation allowances. English concedes their aversion to capital gains tax is purely the politics of it. 'It is not an economic argument, it's like [free] student loans – the middle class likes this stuff; don't mess with it. We were setting out to achieve politically viable ongoing change.'

They did make one daring decision that year, raising the rate of GST to 15 per cent, effective from 1 October 2010, which would almost balance the revenue lost in income tax cuts. Though the GST increase was in breach of a pre-election promise, it had been recommended by the tax working group and the Treasury had been urging them to shift more of the tax burden from 'mobile' sources such as business and workers, who can leave the country, to property and consumption, which have to stay here. The GST rise was announced as early as February 2010 but it was overshadowed in the May budget by the new income tax rates: a four-step scale from 10.5 per cent on the first $14,000, 17.5 per cent up to $48,000, 30 per cent to $70,000, and a top rate reduced from 38 per cent to 33 per cent. A lower company rate of 28 per cent would apply from the following year. Any revenue the government lost from company tax would be more than recovered from the depreciation changes and tax-loss loopholes it was closing.

The opposition condemned the cuts as favouring the better-off, and argued that the flat GST falls more heavily on those who have to spend a higher proportion of their income. A post-budget Colmar Brunton Poll had the government down five points to 49 per cent but a month later TV3 Reid found it back at 55 per cent. Key's popularity was given a different word in the country's leading business circles. They were calling it 'political capital', and with the worst of the recession behind, they wanted him to start spending it on policies that might be unpopular but would improve the economy in the long run. They had been disappointed at his surrender to protests against exploratory drilling for minerals in the Coromandel and other conservation areas. They welcomed legislation allowing new workers to be hired on 90-day trials but worried that, unlike Australia and the United States, New Zealand was in line for a carbon emissions trading scheme that would put additional cost on some sectors.

The recovery was still delicate, business and consumer confidence still low. The government was still trying to stimulate activity by running large budget deficits and adding to public debt. At the beginning of September, the country reeled at the collapse of South Canterbury Finance owing nearly $1.8 billion. Unlike the finance company collapses of 2007, this one was covered by the retail deposit guarantee given to the financial sector at the height of the global financial crisis in 2008. South Canterbury's debenture holders would be paid off at a cost to the public of $1.6 billion. It was small comfort that the government expected to recover the bulk of its outlay in sales of the company's assets over the next three or four years. As the first claim on the banking guarantee, the company's failure carried a chilling echo of the crisis two years earlier.

But within days of that collapse, another event in Canterbury would overwhelm economic concerns and dominate John Key's workload for years to come.

CHAPTER FIFTEEN

Seismic and Fiscal Shocks

Deep under the Canterbury Plains in the pre-dawn darkness of 4 September 2010, a sliver of the planet's outer crust moved. Every person in Christchurch was jolted awake by a force that felt and sounded like a train hitting their house. As the ground heaved and bedrooms shook, it hardly seemed possible that a building could be left standing. Once the shaking stopped and people ventured outside, the night was still black. They could only wait and shudder in dread at what the dawn might reveal.

Later that Saturday when the city had taken stock, it counted itself lucky. The earthquake, recorded at magnitude 7.1 on the Richter scale, had cracked old stone buildings and masonry had fallen from their gables. Land near the Avon River had slumped towards the water, causing the houses to buckle beyond repair. Numerous streets were no longer level, sewers had been ruptured, but no lives had been lost. For many residents, the worst of the first earthquake was the stinking mud of 'liquefaction' from shaken soil. How much worse it could have been, everyone agreed, if the quake had been centred nearer the city, shallower, and happened not at night but on a working day when people were out and about, in or near those stone buildings.

Two months later, on the other side of the Southern Alps, a disaster did claim lives. This time nature was not to blame. Nobody yet knows what caused the explosion in a small, two-year-old coal mine tunnelled into the rugged Paparoa Range on the West Coast. Rescue services rushed to the entrance of the Pike River Mine that Friday afternoon, 19 November 2010. Two young miners had made their way out. The Mines Rescue crew waited in hope that more of those working underground might emerge. Likely methane levels in the mine made it unsafe to enter. The next day and for three more days, families of 29 miners waited in hope that some sort of rescue attempt might be possible. On 24 November a second explosion ended any hope they might be alive.

John Key could do little more than set up a royal commission of inquiry. As it got under way, attention turned back to Christchurch where aftershocks from the September quake were continuing. A jolt on Boxing Day was particularly sharp. Geologists warned that aftershocks could continue for a year and could be nearly as powerful as the original quake. But even they were astonished at the forces that hit the city on 22 February 2011.

It was only magnitude 6.3 but it was close to the surface and close to the city centre. This time it did happen in daylight, in lunch hour on a summer Tuesday. The shops and cafés were busy, city workers were out in the sunshine and some no doubt were checking their watches at 12.51 p.m. in Cashel mall or on the Avon's grassy banks, thinking they had a few precious minutes left before returning to work. The seismic wave that knocked them over at that moment had the greatest ground acceleration ever recorded in New Zealand, vertically and horizontally, 1.8 times the force of gravity.

People were thrown from chairs; bricks and building stone were heaved skyward. ChristChurch Cathedral's familiar spire tumbled to a pile of rubble. As masonry toppled into streets and shop verandahs crumpled over footpaths and parked vehicles, people fled the central city on foot. Those who were injured were helped to first-aid stations quickly set up in open squares. By evening the central area was deserted except for fire crews and the first Civil Defence search-and-rescue teams looking for any survivors amid the debris.

At times such as these a city and a country needs to see a leader. As New York mayor Rudy Giuliani exemplified on 11 September 2001, people need a familiar face, a figure of calm and a frank summary of the few known facts to give reassurance that some sort of order is being restored. Christchurch mayor Bob Parker had met this need so well after the September quake that, against earlier predictions, he had been re-elected in October. On 22 February he was equally visible. So was John Key, who flew to the city as soon as news of the quake started to break in the early afternoon. On television news bulletins he gave the country an estimate of the death toll (65) he had received from police and said, 'We may be witnessing New Zealand's darkest day.'

The final death toll was 185. The central business district was in ruins. The eastern suburbs that had suffered the worst damage in the first quake were hit again. Weary residents got out their shovels and started clearing the liquefaction muck for a second time. Then, many of those who had made insurance claims from the first quake had a second round of paperwork to do. At least they were acquainted with the procedure now, and the sometimes conflicting answers they could expect from the state Earthquake Commission (EQC), insurer of their land, and the companies holding their home and contents insurance. The new problem left by the second quake was the city centre. All of it was being cordoned off.

The day after the quake, Key and Gerry Brownlee met the Canterbury Employers' Chamber of Commerce chief executive, Peter Townsend, and decided to fund every displaced business for eight to 10 weeks, paying 80 per cent of their wages.

> I went to the officials and said, 'Look, we are going to do this.' They looked at me like I was a Martian and said, 'It's not good public policy, Prime Minister. We don't do things this way.' I said, 'I don't care. How are they going to pay their bills?' It cost us $250 million but I still get people coming up to me in Christchurch saying they have 10 employees and they wouldn't be here now if we hadn't done that.

The speedy relocation of central Christchurch business was remarkable – of the 54,000 people who received the employment subsidy in February, only 450 were still on the unemployment benefit in June. Firms were able to move to the largely unscathed western and southwestern areas of the city.

Meanwhile, the entire city's land damage from both quakes was being surveyed by EQC's engineers, Tonkin & Taylor Ltd, to assess where it was practical for houses to stay and services to be restored. When the map was published, after yet another unnerving aftershock in June, most properties had a green light. The 'red zone' was largely a strip through the eastern suburbs near the Avon and its estuary. The government offered to buy all insured red-zone homes at their value in 2007, the peak of the property boom, and take over their insurance claims.

———————

No restoration appeared possible at Pike River. The royal commission reported in June. With the mine still unsafe to enter, the inquiry could only work on external evidence. It found the mining venture had been based on insufficient geological information, and suffered construction delays and escalating costs before it opened in 2008. It had only one vent and its main fan was inside the mine – 'a world first', commented the commission.

In November 2010 the company had been under pressure to increase production and raise more capital. It had started using a water jet at the coal face, which required expert operation to avoid releasing too much methane. As coal was cut away, the roof of the void was unsupported and liable to collapse, sending methane through the mine. A collapse had occurred on 30 October. Since hydro-mining began, dangerously high methane readings had been recorded most days, but the information was not properly assessed at the time and the response had been inadequate.

Equally inadequate was the mine's supervision by the Department of Labour. In 2012 the commission reported on wider issues. It found the department ought to have prohibited hydro-mining until a second exit was tunnelled. The only egress, apart from the portal 2 kilometres back, was a ladder in the 110-metre ventilation shaft. The commission reported that mine inspectors did not have the system, training or time to assess Pike's safety information. 'This was not a case of individual fault, but of departmental failure to resource, manage and adequately support a diminished mining inspectorate.' Minister of Labour Kate Wilkinson took formal responsibility and resigned, keeping her other portfolios. But the real fault probably lay with legislation from 20 years earlier, in the deregulatory era, which reduced the role of mine inspectors.

The Labour Department was absorbed into a new Ministry of Business, Innovation and Employment which brought an action against Pike River Coal in the Greymouth District Court for breaches of health and safety. In July 2013, Judge Jane Farish convicted the company and ordered it to pay the families $3.41 million, which would have given $110,000 to the family of each victim and the two survivors, Russell Smith and Daniel Rockhouse. Pike River Coal said it was in receivership and could pay only $5000 to each. Judge Farish accused the company of a 'total lack of remorse' and noted Pike River's biggest secured shareholder, New Zealand Oil & Gas, had posted a profit the previous year of $19.9 million.

The families received standard ACC payouts totalling $5 million, plus a share of public donations totalling $6,288,617 – an average of just under $217,000 each. In November 2013, Labour leader David Cunliffe promised a Labour government would pay the families the sum awarded against the company and seek reimbursement from Pike River Coal's directors and shareholders using 'the power of the office of the Prime Minister'. The sitting Prime Minister, meanwhile, had pledged $10 million for a tentative plan to re-enter the mine, or at least go as far as a rockfall in the entry tunnel where the families believed some of the 29 may have been. However, Key said it was his advice that the plan was 'very unlikely' to be deemed safe.

The families' spokesman, Bernie Monk, replied, 'How can they say that until we get down there? I think that's a very unfair comment as well . . . I think they've been poorly advised.'

Key was careful to say nothing to give the families false hope, without being insensitive to their hope against hope that any mortal remains could have survived.

———————

While not much could be done at Pike River, more definite plans were being drawn up for rebuilding the Christchurch central business district, still behind a cordon of mesh fences. The first time Fletcher Building's infrastructure head, Mark Binns, went inside the cordon he was astonished. 'It was a sobering and humbling experience to see the devastation. It is just massive,' he said at the time. 'It is a game-changer and needs a rethink, I think.' He urged the government to set up a special agency of 'high-quality bureaucrats' to take over the city's reconstruction, drawing advice from engineers, planners and building experts. 'When we had the first quake there was a view we may be able to do all the work just with Canterbury people. That has changed. There will need to be workers from outside Canterbury. It is just a question of how far afield we will have to go.' At the end of March 2011, the government set up the Canterbury Earthquake Recovery Authority with wide powers to bypass laws and regulations. 'CERA' quickly became a household name in Christchurch.

Of the 185 who died in the city on 22 February, 133 were

in two buildings: Canterbury Television (CTV) and Pyne Gould Corporation (PGC). Of the other 52, only four died inside a building. Considering the ground forces that hit the city that day, it is a wonder that more multi-storey buildings did not topple. Most of them were damaged beyond economic repair and have since been demolished, but they stood up well enough that day to let people escape. They withstood a shock greater than even modern buildings are designed to absorb. So did New Zealand's economy.

Economists apply the word 'shock' to any event that upsets the normal ebb and flow of confidence of business and consumers. When an economy goes into shock the consequences fall on the public finances with a drop in tax revenue and a rise in social welfare expenses. The budget goes into deficit which adds to the public debt. The economic equivalent of a building's shock-absorber is low public debt. If the country has been well governed with balanced budgets in good times, it can afford to cushion a shock for a few years without its debt becoming a crippling burden and a credit risk. New Zealand has been well governed for 30 years by both National and Labour parties.

But in 2011 John Key's government had already let deficits and debt deepen for two years to absorb the shock of the global financial crisis. Before the February earthquake it had been planning to start tightening its spending. After the quake, finance minister Bill English told a capital markets conference the government would borrow another $10 billion to cover its expected share of the cost. The deficit that year would be a massive $18.3 billion, adding another 9.2 per cent of GDP to the public debt.

The day that Fletcher's Mark Binns had gone inside the central-city cordon he made a rough calculation that the cost of the rebuild would be $20 billion, not the $15 billion estimated by Treasury. New Zealand's total economy at that time had a gross domestic product (GDP) of just under $200 billion. About 15 per cent of that came from Canterbury. An economist for investment bank Goldman Sachs, Philip Borkin, thought the possibility of a credit downgrade was real 'due to the increased pressure on the government's books from the costs of the earthquake'. Later in March, Moody's Investors Service put New Zealand on 'negative outlook'. By then the global insurance pool was facing the costs of a second destructive earthquake in Japan that had caused a devastating tsunami.

Treasury's initial estimates of the costs of the rebuild, $15 billion, with about $8.8 billion falling on the taxpayer, were indeed way below the mark. The budget of 2012 put the cost at $20 billion, English calling it 'the largest and most complex economic project in New Zealand's history'. The following year the cost had risen to $40 billion with the government contribution alone approaching $15 billion. By then, though, the economy was growing with help from the rebuild and the budget was on course for a small surplus in 2014–15, a year earlier than projected before the February earthquake.

––––––––

The Key government's control of public expenditure through both financial and seismic shocks has been remarkably painless. Key gives all the credit to Bill English. As a junior Treasury officer before entering Parliament at age 28, English is a rare finance minister who has seen the public service from the inside. He was convinced there were savings to be found without cuts to services, by giving the departments clear, concrete, measureable targets. They would be as specific as: increase immunisation, reduce rheumatic fever, reduce criminal reoffending, increase the NCEA Level 2 pass rate and reduce long-term welfare dependency. An actuarial valuation system has been devised to measure the long-term welfare liability, as English explains.

> The fundamental driver of the government's budgetary costs is social dysfunction. It is not health, not education, it is people whose lives are messy. If you take a longer-term view about fixing problems, not a short-term view about cutting programmes, you find out that what works for the community [also] works for the government's books. If we stop a prisoner reoffending we save $90,000. If we have a group of seven- to nine-year-olds who are going to cost $750 million by the time they turn 30, we need more health checks, healthy homes, social workers in schools. John has created permission for a centre-right government to talk about public services positively.

The targets were announced in February 2012. Key was also keen to make them public but many in the cabinet were nervous. English thinks he and Key came within a week of losing the argument. 'Politicians never like to go out and say, "This is what we want to achieve", in any definitive way.' Too much can go wrong. 'The more ministers looked at the list we were proposing, the more uneasy they got. I was thinking, "If we don't get this thing through this week it's going to disappear."' They got it through and Key announced the list publicly. They knew it would not make news until they missed a target, but the intended audience for the targets was not the press, it was the public service, and English says the message was received.

> It has transformed public-sector thinking. You've got
> to remember the public sector gets bigger by feeding
> off problems; solving them makes it smaller. They have
> developed a great capacity for measuring problems.
> There is a saying that the Labour Party these days
> represents not the working class but the measuring
> class. They just measure things endlessly. They are big
> complex organisations, and – this is the bit the Prime
> Minister understands because he has been in large
> organisations – they don't know what they actually
> do. Right down to middle management, they don't
> know, they are all managing up. They know where the
> minister's office is and how big the cash spout is. If you
> tell them to save $100 million they will do all sorts
> of random amputations. We have given them time to
> understand what they do. The targets mean they have
> to go and find out what their front-line people do –
> what they *actually* do.

After two 'zero budgets' (sub-inflation 1.5 per cent
increases in spending), the economy has weathered the
shocks from Canterbury and is enjoying a stimulus from
the rebuild that is a mixed blessing. It means that a great
deal of capital and resources, amounting to one fifth of the
entire economy, are going into the building industry which
is not an internationally trading sector. It does not offer the
country a stronger economy in the long run.

Three years on from the February quake, the Christchurch central business district has a blueprint for a low-
rise resurrection within a green frame. It is hoped new
government buildings will encourage commerce to return

in clusters around them. Two hospitals are being repaired and enlarged; a justice 'precinct' has been funded. A sports stadium and convention centre also feature on the plan. Wayne Eagleson rates the rebuild as one of Key's three main aims in government, along with education standards and welfare reform. 'We would have him in Christchurch at least once every couple of weeks. He spends a lot of his time thinking about Christchurch and working with Gerry and Bill [English] on it. He has a real view that it can be a better city than it was.'

It was the city of John Key's childhood and education. One of his sisters still lives there. Bronagh admits she is still a Christchurch girl at heart. 'I like Auckland but Christchurch is always home. It was a great place to grow up and I love going home to see family.' When Auckland plays Canterbury, just quietly, she is red and black.

CHAPTER SIXTEEN

Commanding Trust

At the dawn of election year 2011, John Key made an announcement that silenced those in business circles who thought he lacked the backbone to put his popularity on the line for the sake of the economy. He announced a programme of asset sales. By doing so when he did, he displayed far more courage than reformers of yesteryear who had never put their more daring reforms to a popular vote until after the fact. Key announced his programme before an election and asked for a mandate. It was breathtaking.

'Privatisation' has been an unspeakable word in politics for as long as anyone can remember. People feel they have a personal stake in public property and do not like losing any part of it. Even the drastic reform programme of the fourth Labour government did not include privatisation until after it had been re-elected. Its cabinet first issued a list of likely sales in mid-1988, and did so to reassure finance markets it was holding course after David Lange's break with Roger Douglas. Had Lange stayed the course, it is doubtful that Douglas could have convinced the cabinet to go further than its corporatisation of public services as 'state-owned enterprises'. Asset sales begun by Labour were eagerly continued by the National government of the 1990s, adding to the public discontent in that decade, but they were firmly renounced by Helen Clark during her nine years in power. Her government bought back Air New Zealand to save it from a disastrous investment decision in Australia, and renationalised the railways after two private owners had failed to make the network economic. Privatisation was ruled out by John Key for his first term. In January 2011 it was proposed by Bill English as a solution to a debt problem.

> In 2010, debt was rising rapidly and we'd had the first earthquake. I was thinking, 'If we don't do something this could really get away on us.' We had to knock $10 billion out of the budget. The first time I raised [asset sales] in cabinet, they laughed. People don't underestimate John Key now but they did then.

When Key announced the programme he made it as palatable as he could. No more than 49 per cent of the chosen assets would be floated on the share market. The state would retain the majority holding. It was only a partial privatisation, or, as he preferred, a 'mixed ownership model', and the initial public offering would be restricted to New Zealanders. Small investors would be first in the queue.

Public opinion was not appeased. The assets he proposed to float included three big electricity generating companies whose hydro dams, thermal and geothermal plants were among the most visible and valued symbols of national wealth. The hydro projects, in particular, had been highly publicised and celebrated at each stage of their construction in the post-war decades of public investment. In the 1990s they were divided among four companies carved out of the state-owned Electricity Corporation by the previous National government when it put the industry on a competitive footing. One of the companies, Contact Energy, had been sold before the Shipley government lost office. It was logical to put the rest on the market, though Key did not put it that way.

Typically, he tried to make his case to the public in accounting rather than economic terms. The government needed to release some capital for other needs. It had been borrowing heavily to help the country through the recession and global financial crisis and now it faced the cost of earthquake repairs. It was going to hold departmental spending very tight for the next few years but it would need to extract some cash from its balance sheet too. It believed it could release $5–7 billion from the sale of shares in Meridian Energy, Genesis Energy, Mighty River Power, its coal-mining company Solid Energy and Air New Zealand.

It mentioned other benefits: the stocks would give the share market a much-needed boost, more New Zealanders might become business investors, and the state-owned companies would perform better under the active scrutiny of brokers, fund managers and other serious investors. The last-mentioned is the essence of the economic case for privatisation, yet Key and English never made it strongly. They would offer it almost as an afterthought, referring vaguely to 'share market discipline'. They preferred to deal in bookkeeping arguments and most people never bought them.

A TV3 Reid Research Poll soon after the asset sales announcement found 80 per cent opposed to them. A *Herald*-DigiPoll survey in May found more than 62 per cent opposed. In July, DigiPoll measured opposition at 57 per cent, including 40 per cent of those who intended to vote National. A week before that poll Labour had shown matching courage in deciding to go to the election with a capital gains tax – the first time in memory that a major party has done so. National hardly uttered a word of criticism, which suggests a capital gains tax had some powerful support in its caucus too. One old bogey of New Zealand politics may have been laid to rest. When voters were asked which policy they would prefer as a means of reducing government debt, 43 per cent of the DigiPoll sample chose a capital gains tax, against 34 per cent for asset sales.

Events over the next two years would undermine the financial rationale for the sales. A fall in the world price of aluminium cast a cloud over the future of Southland's Tiwai Point smelter which uses 14 per cent of all the power generated in New Zealand. The smelter company, a subsidiary of the global mineral giant Rio Tinto, was trying to renegotiate its future power price with the supplier, Meridian. If they could not agree on a price that would keep the smelter running, the market would be massively oversupplied.

The implications for the value of the companies about to be floated were so dire that the government provided the smelter with a $30 million subsidy to keep it going. Then, on the eve of the first float, the Labour and Green parties jointly announced they would take control of the wholesale electricity market if elected. Despite it all, shares were issued in Mighty River Power at a good price for the government, less so for the buyers. The price soon plummeted and the next public offerings, of Meridian and Genesis, had to be sweetened at additional public cost. The share market had a glut of electricity stock and the financial gain to the government was less than it might have been if the programme had been more gradual.

In the end the case for proceeding with the asset sales was economic rather than financial. It was a rare political opportunity to make virtually all of the economy's electricity supply responsive to active shareholders and commercially accountable for its costs, investments and competitive results.

But all of that was in the future. Despite the unpopularity of asset sales in every poll before the 2011 election, the subject was having no discernible impact on voters' intentions. Support for both National and Key personally continued to soar above 50 per cent. Key was the preferred Prime Minister of 67 per cent in DigiPoll's May sample and 70.6 per cent in July. Most people trusted John Key even if they did not like what he proposed to do.

If there was going to be any doubt that the election would give him a mandate, the Labour Party dispelled it. Back in January, on the day the privatisation programme was announced, Labour leader Phil Goff had declared the election would be 'a referendum on asset sales'. For the rest of the year Labour clung to the belief that Key had made a monumental mistake. With Goff barely polling in double figures, Labour had little else going for it. As November approached, Labour took its leader off its campaign billboards, replacing him with a single message: no asset sales.

The election was an overwhelming endorsement. National increased its share of the vote – a rare achievement for a party in power in New Zealand. National's vote had last risen in office at the snap election following the 1951 waterfront dispute, 10 years before John Key was born. Bill English, a year younger than Key, was not surprised the asset sales programme did them no damage. 'I knew it would be unpopular but I didn't think it was a vote-shifter. More important, John didn't think it was a vote-shifter.' As English explains, governments do their own intensive polling and sometimes discover opposition to a supposedly unpopular policy does not run deep.

> If you poll our voters they will say, 'We don't think it is a good idea', but that is not because they don't think it's a good idea, it's because it's unpopular. It is not as if we ever went to a National Party meeting or a chamber of commerce and they said, 'Don't do that.' They'd say, 'Why are you doing that?' A lot of punters, our base, didn't get Working for Families cut, didn't get super changed, didn't lose interest-free student loans, didn't get small-government rhetoric and the hairy-chested reform stuff, but they had to get something. They had to get some red meat from moderate John.

Key had his mandate when he greeted cheering election-night supporters for a second time at Auckland's SkyCity Convention Centre on 26 November 2011, but that venue would put public trust in him to another test in his second term.

Nearly six months before the 2011 election, Key had announced that SkyCity was the preferred bidder to build, own and operate a 3500-seat convention centre of international standard in Auckland. The casino's bid was preferred over several others for 350 million reasons, all of them dollars. Unlike the others, SkyCity would require no public funds. It was proposing to carry the $350 million cost entirely – in return for a licence extension and the right to install more gaming tables and poker machines. The numbers would be matters of negotiation before the deal was finalised.

Not much more was heard on the subject before the election, but the following year it erupted in a blitz of headlines about problem gambling, especially on 'pokies'. The deal threatened to reverse a sinking lid on pokie machines in Auckland since 2003 when the Labour government empowered councils to stop a proliferation of pokies in pubs.

The Problem Gambling Foundation predicted an upsurge in addiction and questioned whether the casino was a safer gambling environment than clubs and pubs. Incidents involving abandoned children at the casino had nearly tripled in two years. Key believed casinos were generally safer and less likely to encourage casual gambling by those who could least afford it. 'Pokie machines typically prey on low socio-economic groups. There's a high proliferation of them in West Auckland and South Auckland. At least with a casino it's a much more determined action to go there.'

Most people were not persuaded. A DigiPoll survey in May 2012 showed 40.3 per cent disapproved of the pokie deal under any circumstances, 37.7 per cent did not mind so long as the number of poker machines across the city dropped, while less than 20 per cent approved regardless.

In June, questions were raised about Key's personal encouragement of a SkyCity bid and the Office of the

Auditor-General began an inquiry. It was a potent issue for a Prime Minister who opposition parties believed vulnerable to impressions that he was too close to corporate leaders. They constantly accused him of 'cronyism' or 'looking after his mates'. SkyCity's unsuccessful rivals were not much concerned that Key had talked to the casino along the way. Ngati Whatua chief executive Tiwana Tibble said, 'I lobbied the PM, I went and saw him a couple of times. It's a $350 million contract, that's what people do. They don't just stick a tender in the envelope and hope for the best.' Nevertheless, while the now year-long negotiations with SkyCity would continue, nothing would be announced until the Audit Office issued its report.

Deputy Auditor-General Phillippa Smith produced her findings in February 2013, and while she found nothing wrong with the Prime Minister's discussions with the casino, and nor did she express disapproval of the principle that a social policy might be traded for an economic asset, she was concerned that rival tenders were not given the same opportunity.

The deal was finalised and announced in May by Economic Development Minister Steven Joyce, not Key. Auckland would get an international-class convention centre now estimated to cost $402 million and inject $90 million a year into the economy. SkyCity would be able to install 230 additional pokie machines which critics calculated would produce 184 extra problem gamblers at an annual social cost of $6.6 million. Most people were not impressed. A nationwide DigiPoll sample in June recorded opposition to the deal at 61.5 per cent.

But National's support remained around 47 per cent, slightly above its vote at the election, and Key was still the preferred Prime Minister of 63 per cent. The trust

ABOVE: Key with nine-month-old Harry Baxter at Mission Bay, Auckland, during the 2011 election campaign.

NEW ZEALAND HERALD

LEFT: Preparing for the Pole. The Prime Minister gets his kit before a visit to Antarctica, January 2013.

NEW ZEALAND HERALD

TOP: At the Chunuk Bair memorial on the Gallipoli Peninsula, Anzac Day 2010.
PRIME MINISTER'S STAFF COLLECTION

BOTTOM: Our darkest day. Key prepares to go on evening television news bulletins from
Christchurch after the earthquake on 22 February 2011. PRIME MINISTER'S STAFF COLLECTION

TOP: A 'pull aside', diplomats call them. Key grabs a moment with President Barack Obama at Nuclear Security Summit in South Korea, March 2012. NATIONAL PARTY PHOTO

BOTTOM: Australian and New Zealand Prime Ministers Tony Abbott and John Key with former US President Bill Clinton at the funeral of Nelson Mandela, December 2013. PRIME MINISTER'S STAFF COLLECTION

TOP: Inner circle. Key with senior cabinet ministers Steven Joyce (left) and Bill English in the meeting room adjoining the Prime Minister's office in the Beehive. PRIME MINISTER'S STAFF COLLECTION

BOTTOM: Cheeky. The Prime Minister is greeted at Auckland's Big Gay Out in Coyle Park, Point Chevalier, Auckland, February 2013. *HERALD ON SUNDAY*

Key commanded was all the more remarkable for the fact that he had faced many more troubles than these in his second term.

Key's troubles had started during the election campaign. Like Clark at her second election when she was ambushed on television by 'Corngate', Key lost his composure over an incident the press soon christened 'Teagate'. A freelance photographer had left a live recording device in its case on the table in the Newmarket café where Key and ACT's new Epsom candidate, John Banks, were staging a cup of tea together as a sign to National voters in Epsom that they should give their party a partner. Key did not discover the recording device until after he and Banks had exchanged some candid views, including the observation that Winston Peters' elderly supporters were dying out. The recording was given to the *Herald on Sunday* and it treated the conversation as private, seeking Key's permission to publish a transcript. He not only refused permission, he called in the police, thereby creating a story that dominated the rest of the election campaign. Peters capitalised, getting his party over the 5 per cent threshold and returning to Parliament with eight seats.

Key's greatest political attribute had deserted him. For the first time he had let a trivial incident matter, and it continued to gnaw at him. Months later, when talking about it, his cheerful demeanour would change. He remained deeply disturbed, not by his own response, but by the recording. He did not believe it accidental, and neither did the police. Assistant Commissioner Malcolm Burgess said investigators believed it was at least reckless but more likely deliberate. Key settled for a letter of regret from the cameraman.

> The tea tape stuff wound me up – I probably shouldn't
> have let it. It is one of the few times that something
> ever has. It was a violation of trust between me and
> the press gallery. I shouldn't have let it hit me so deeply
> but anyway I did and that's life. The public didn't care
> about it.

By March of 2012, the first year of his second term was not going smoothly. A Chinese company's bid to buy the Crafer family's 16 farms was testing public acceptance of foreign, or maybe just Asian, investment. The High Court found fault with the Overseas Investment Office's initial approval of the sale. On other fronts, the asset sales were made subject to Treaty claims at the insistence of the Maori Party and the power company floats would have to be reconciled with rights of iwi to have questions of freshwater ownership considered. A National Party member, Bronwyn Pullar, was telling the press about an ACC spreadsheet sent to her by mistake with other people's file numbers on it. The press were calling it a 'massive security breach'. ACC minister Nick Smith resigned when it became known he had written a letter in support of Pullar's accident claim.

But Key's problems were just beginning. Back in January the police had swooped with paramilitary force on a sprawling mansion at Coatesville. The occupant, a big, baby-faced German who had made a fortune on a file-sharing website, was wanted in the United States to answer copyright charges. Kim Dotcom was not willing to go. His Megaupload site was taken down and Dotcom spent a month in custody before he was bailed to fight extradition. He felt let down when he wanted help from former Auckland mayor John Banks, who had replaced Rodney Hide as ACT MP for Epsom, and let it be known he had donated $50,000 to Banks's unsuccessful mayoral re-election campaign in 2010. He mentioned the sum had been divided in two, at Banks's suggestion, so that it could remain anonymous.

Banks pleaded severe memory loss. An initial police investigation found he had personally solicited the money recorded as anonymous on an electoral return he had signed, but it found no evidence he had knowingly filed a false return. Key preferred not to read the police report. By then the Dotcom case had presented him with a greater problem.

Seriously rich, with a personal fortune estimated at that time to be about four times Key's own wealth, Dotcom had hired a top legal team led by the highly respected Paul Davison QC. They were winning in court on procedural issues over the January raid and had discovered that New Zealand's external intelligence agency, the Government Communications Security Bureau, had monitored Dotcom at the request of the police. The GCSB's governing statute at that time did not allow it to spy on New Zealand citizens, which included an immigrant granted residency.

Intelligence agencies are always part of a Prime Minister's portfolio and Key blamed the illegal operation on 'brain fade' at the GCSB. He issued an apology to Dotcom but it did no good. The story would only get worse for Key. Having denied any personal knowledge of the GCSB's role in Dotcom's arrest, he had to admit a month later that it had been mentioned to him when he visited the GCSB offices not long after the raid. In Parliament the opposition howled that it was the Prime Minister who was suffering brain fade.

To the public, Dotcom and the GCSB was a sideshow, but at the end of September, John Armstrong noted the

rising spirits of opposition parties as two polls showed a
slight narrowing of National's lead. 'What has changed – if
only briefly – is the Prime Minister's demeanour,' he wrote.
'His natural effervescence and self-confidence seemed to
desert him in the House. His normally precise answers to
questions sounded vague and uncertain. On Wednesday
afternoon, Key was required to return to the debating
chamber to correct one of his answers – a rare lapse for a
Prime Minister.'

It had been a frustrating year, easily his most difficult
year in politics to that point. Besides all the minor
issues, the asset sales programme had been delayed by a
case brought by the New Zealand Maori Council to the
Waitangi Tribunal, which was then taken through three
courts. Key had not helped matters with a comment on
radio, on the day the tribunal began hearing the case,
that the government could ignore its findings. Schools
had lost patience with a new software system, Novopay,
that had left too many staff with no pay for too long. And
the budget that year had planned to increase school class
sizes. Principals appealed to parents and Key reversed the
cabinet's decision as quickly as a good currency trader
abandons a losing position.

He had always backed his ability to stay focused on
the issues that really matter in politics and ignore those
that might make news for a week but will be deservedly
forgotten a week later. This year, though, trivia seemed to
take on a life of its own. When he went home at the end of
2012 he had a quiet discussion with Bronagh.

> We had a talk about it after four years. Just kicked the
> tyres – are we still committed to all this? I used to
> worry about losing. Losing feels like failure and I don't

kinda like failure. But after a while, I thought, 'Look, I really believe in what we are doing.' Sure, I could walk away, but the test of being a successful Prime Minister in my mind is doing the best job I could do in the circumstances we faced. People have been writing this stuff about the GCSB and criticising us for it, but two agents made the decision that they got wrong and I had to carry it as the minister. Nothing I could do about that. Didn't know about it, didn't authorise it, wasn't part of it, you are just there. I don't beat myself up over that stuff because it has just come as part of the job. So we had a view – Bronagh was much stronger on it than I was – that I would be running away, and why would I do that?

As Bronagh puts it, 'You don't lose if you have done the best job you can do and see it through to the point that you have done all you can.'

They would go to Hawaii again. He would have a break, recharge, do some thinking, and when they returned, he would start the New Year with a decision that would startle his ministers and revitalise his government.

CHAPTER SEVENTEEN

Not a Job for Life

When John Key returned from holiday in the New Year of 2013, he fired two ministers for nothing in particular that they had done. Kate Wilkinson and Phil Heatley would have had no inkling of their fate when they were summoned to the ninth floor. Key calls every minister to his office at the beginning of a year for a discussion of the year ahead in their portfolio.

> I called Kate and asked her to come and see me. When she came in, we sat down and I said, 'Look, you've done a great job as a minister but it's over.' She said, 'You mean you're giving me some other portfolio?' And I said, 'No, I'm not giving you any portfolios.' She said, 'What have I done wrong?' I said, 'Nothing. You have done four years and I want to refresh.' I said the same thing to Phil.

Surely it wasn't quite that blunt? 'Yes,' he says, 'it was.' There is no anger or anguish on his face when he says so, no sentiment at all. It was a dispassionate political calculation. 'You gotta keep refreshing.' It was something he had to do a lot at Merrill Lynch – too much, he thinks.

> Merrill was a bit schizophrenic and sometimes they'd be in a crisis and they would make wholesale lay-offs. I'd say, 'This is crazy – these people are making you money.' But you gotta keep bringing good people through. That was important at Merrill too. Look, it's never great fun and it's not something you'd want to do. In the end it comes with the job.

He had a caucus of 59 MPs and a ministry of 24, of whom 20 could be in the cabinet. 'All [59] are ambitious, all A-type personalities, otherwise they wouldn't be here.' Many who have not made the cabinet are also quitting at the 2014 election, several on Key's advice. 'Some of the hardest conversations are with people who haven't got there and I've just said, "Look, honestly, it won't happen."'

When word of Wilkinson's and Heatley's fate filtered down through the Beehive, Wayne Eagleson says, 'You could hear a pin drop around this building.' Ministers remembered that when they were in opposition Key used to say he intended to give as many competent people as he could a chance to be in cabinet. Ministers should not assume they would be there for a full term. Clearly, he meant it. 'Backbenchers looked at it and realised this is a guy who actually will reward performance and there may be chances,' says Eagleson. 'It is good for the team dynamic – it keeps everybody working pretty hard.'

Key brought Nikki Kaye and Simon Bridges into the cabinet that year. The following year when Chris Tremain, a minister outside the cabinet, intended to retire at the election, Key replaced him early with Peseta Sam Lotu-Iiga, National's first minister of Pacific Island descent.

The large turnover of National MPs at the 2014 election may encourage a return to the party's culture of the Holyoake era when being a member of Parliament was not a career but a public service by people who had been successful, or at least had years of useful experience, in farming, business or professions in the private sector. Parliament needs young people too, but under John Key they are not encouraged to regard a safe seat as a sinecure for life.

One or two successful ministers appear to have taken a cue from Key's own career to make a midlife switch. Minister of Justice Simon Power left after the first term and has a high executive rank at Westpac bank. Minister of Health Tony Ryall, who has kept a difficult state service remarkably quiet, is retiring from politics in 2014 at age 49.

What about the Prime Minister himself? For years, there has been conjecture that Key will not stay in politics very long, or at least will retire before his time is up. Where does that rumour come from? 'The Labour Party,' he laughs. He assumes it has something to do with the fact that he does not need the salary and a suspicion that he wanted to become Prime Minister only to 'tick the box, put it in my CV'.

John Key will be 53 at the 2014 election. He has aged visibly in six years but his frequent trips overseas continue to attest to his health and enjoyment of his role. Reporters know how punishing those trips are. When any minister travels, New Zealand diplomats in the host country make full use of their time. Talks with various counterparts, often for just 15 or 30 minutes at a time, fill their day and frequently their evening. Every meeting, no matter how short, requires a briefing and a clear focus on issues of interest to New Zealand. When a Prime Minister travels, he or she is usually accompanied by New Zealand media and must also stay in touch with any issue of political moment in the news at home. The days must be dizzying and the jet lag exhausting. Key seems to relish it.

Back home, he usually sleeps three nights a week in the lonely splendour of Wellington's Premier House. 'Splendour' should be the right word but it is not. Premier House is a Category I historic place and, inside, it looks like it. It was the residence of premiers from the 1860s to the 1930s, when Michael Joseph Savage preferred it to be a school for dental nurses. Repossessed and renovated in the 1980s, its furnishings remain minimal. As a state reception centre, it is no better than tidy. The plain walls and simple painted timber ceilings might be authentic, but the only reason New Zealand does not boast something more suitable is that governments would be accused of spending money on themselves.

His own home in Auckland is protected around the clock by police stationed in a gatehouse. Nobody enters the property or leaves without being observed. The Prime Minister cannot go for a walk to the shops without notifying his security. Key does not seem to mind – as he says, it goes with the job. He and Bronagh do get out to Parnell cafés and restaurants where they are well known. People in the street always want a photo and Bronagh takes the snap. She thinks she now knows every make of camera on the market.

She resisted the 24/7 security at first. 'I'm pretty independent and didn't like the idea. But you find over time that it is quite helpful because New Zealand does know where we live.' Soon after his election in 2008, Key complained that a trade union, Unite, had started picketing his house when he was not there. 'I don't believe it is appropriate to be protesting to my wife and children,' he said, and the demonstrations ceased.

The New Zealand press and public generally respect the privacy of politicians' families, but anything they do that is out of the ordinary or unlawful is liable to attract publicity. That was one of the reasons John Key had a meeting with his sisters and their families when he decided to stand for Parliament. 'He knew it would impact on us, and it has,' says Sue Lazar. 'I never let my boys get outrageously drunk or do drugs. I told them in no uncertain terms, "Do anything like that and you'll be in the paper."'

Key's own children have kept out of the spotlight except for the day the *Herald on Sunday* decided to feature a picture of Stephie (20) apparently naked except for strategically placed items of fast food. It was an art photo from her blog, taken as part of her studies in Paris. Asked about it on his Monday *Breakfast* television appearance, Key laughed. 'We always told her to eat her food, not play with it.' Bronagh was very proud of her daughter.

> She is doing some great work. She was mortified that people would see work that wasn't finished photographic work. They were photos for them to do sketching. Actually it was quite funny because we were keeping an eye on her budget and at one point we saw this big bill for McDonald's and I said, 'What's this? McDonald's hardly cuts the mustard.' She said it was for school. I said, 'Yeah, right.' But when the photo came out it was McDonald's.

Stephie's parents think she will stay in Europe. Part of

the reason she went to France was to be her own person, not simply John Key's daughter. Max is the same, says Bronagh. 'They want to do it on their own.' Max (18), still living with them, is in the second year of a business and law degree at the University of Auckland. Both were children in London but Stephie, the older by two years, has always had a hankering to return. They think she will make her life over there.

Bronagh would like to spend some time in Europe when eventually she gets her husband back from public life. 'I've always wanted to go somewhere and learn a language, maybe Italian. John loves the idea of learning Italian cooking, so maybe it would be great to go somewhere like Italy. I could come home to a sumptuous big meal every evening.'

'Yeah, spag bol,' quips John.

'Garlic bread and spag bol,' Bronagh suggests.

Key says he will probably take company directorships after politics. 'I really like business.' He is adamant he will not be an ambassador anywhere. Despite the evident value of his personality in foreign relations, exemplified by Obama's golf invitation, he has no interest in seeking a diplomatic post.

———

John Key, of course, is not going anywhere for a good while if he can help it. If his prospects depended entirely on him, his popularity and his cautious mode of government would give him every chance of surviving for three or even four terms. Holyoake, whom he admires, had four terms. Like Holyoake, Key believes in never getting ahead of public opinion unless you are sure you can take your supporters with you, as Key did on dealings with Maori and same-sex marriage.

He is a much more popular figure than Holyoake ever was, but Holyoake had only to win elections. Key has to win and hope potential partners can get enough seats to give him a parliamentary majority. Unless he can break the mould of New Zealand politics and National receives more than 50 per cent of the popular vote, every election could be his last.

Winners can be losers under proportional representation, though it has not happened in New Zealand yet. The country has had six elections under MMP since 1996 and politicians with the balance of power have always given it to the party first past the post. One way or another, it is hard to see Key losing power for as long as his popularity lasts. But however long that may be, there will come a time when the tide turns, the public tires of his face and voice and is no longer receptive to his policies and persuasion. When that happens, Key the currency trader could be among the first to sense the sea change, and might not hang around to face defeat. His admission at the end of the previous chapter, 'Losing feels like failure and I don't kinda like failure', is telling.

When that day comes, who in National ranks might succeed him? If he retires in office during the next parliamentary term, the most likely successor could be Steven Joyce, though Bill English might be hungrier for the position. Joyce is the party's nearest replica of Key. Joyce has business credibility, having built up and sold a company, setting himself up financially. He, too, does not need politics for his livelihood. He is calm, authoritative, genial and a more concise communicator than Key. Most importantly, his instincts and judgement are equally sound.

If Key does not step down until he has lost an election, or lost government to a coalition of the second- and third-placed parties, Joyce might retire too. He has never been in opposition, preferring party organisational roles outside Parliament until 2008 when National was clearly coming into power and he took a high place on its list. If National is in opposition when it next changes its leader, its best current contender appears to be Judith Collins. Her combative style and verbal skills, a complete contrast with John Key, might cloud her future in his government but they are ideal for opposition.

You can refresh your team, revitalise its performance, but the same issues can return and become bigger problems. In 2013, Novopay was still failing to pay too many in schools and Steven Joyce was on its case. The power company share floats were at least ready to proceed with Maori court actions behind them, but Tiwai Point and a Labour–Green plan for price control had undermined their value. Any prospect of selling Solid Energy had passed. The company was close to collapse after a plunge in the coal price the previous year. The government had contentiously amended labour law so that Warner Bros. would film *The Hobbit* in New Zealand. And Dotcom, like a tar-baby of politics, was still damaging those who dared touch anything to do with him. The previous year it was Banks; that year it was another of National's partners, Peter Dunne.

John Key had commissioned the cabinet secretary, Rebecca Kitteridge, to investigate the illegal surveillance of Dotcom by the GCSB. Her report, finding the agency had frequently misinterpreted its legislation, was leaked a week earlier than its scheduled release, while Key was on a visit to Japan. He did not welcome the distraction and, on his return, had Eagleson commission an investigation. Parliamentary emails and swipe-card records were checked and suspicion fell on Dunne who had exchanged 86 email messages with the reporter who received the leak, the *Dominion Post*'s Andrea Vance. The government, meanwhile, had put a bill before Parliament that would allow the GCSB to provide police and domestic agencies with data on the communications of citizens and residents.

The GCSB bill faced a wave of concern heightened by a worldwide disclosure of the United States National Security Agency's access to telecommunications logs. The GCSB would have similar powers to keep track of somebody's communications and provide the information to police or domestic intelligence agencies with a warrant for the surveillance. Its own role would also be widened in cyber-security protection. The bill provoked an outcry from lawyers concerned for civil liberties and prompted public meetings as well as submissions to Parliament. Some prominent people spoke out, including Dame Anne Salmond, historian, who wrote:

> The GCSB bill would give the agency sweeping powers with the only effective controls in the hands of politicians. Given the recent record of legislative attacks on human rights in this country, very few New Zealanders could be confident that such powers, if granted, would not be abused for partisan political purposes.

Kim Dotcom, still facing extradition to the United States over his own use of the internet, appeared before the parliamentary committee hearings on the bill, chaired by the Prime Minister. A memorable exchange was replayed on television. Labour leader David Shearer asked Dotcom if he believed Key did not know of him before the Coatesville raid.

'Oh, he knew about me before the raid. I know about that,' said Dotcom.

'I didn't,' said Key.

'You know I know,' said Dotcom.

'I know you don't know actually, but that's fine,' Key replied.

'Why are you turning red, Prime Minister?' Dotcom glared.

'I'm not,' parried Key. 'Why are you sweating?'

'I'm hot,' retorted Dotcom.

Through all this, the government was incurring a flood of protest on a different subject. Primary Industries Minister Nathan Guy was considering a reduction in the permitted snapper catch for recreational fishing. Key told Parliament the public was far more worked up about snapper than the GCSB.

> I wasn't joking. Everywhere I went the first question was about bloody bag limits for snapper. I'd say, 'Don't you want to know about the GCSB?' and they'd say, 'No.' Most people are quite correct in assuming they will never get spied on, and they watch the news, they know there is a small risk something might happen and we have intelligence agencies for a reason. People who feel intensely about it, the John Campbells of this world, the left, the Greens, have had that perspective all their lives. They are very distrusting of the Americans and so on, [but] that is not where most people are at.

Labour's long-struggling leader took the bait. Someone encouraged David Shearer to stand up in the House holding two dead fish as he criticised the proposed bag limit. From National's front bench, Judith Collins asked, 'Which one of those three will last the longest?' Shearer gave up the leadership two days later. His resignation triggered a party election under new rules forced on the Labour caucus by party activists and unions at the annual conference the previous year. Unhappy with the caucus's choice of Shearer, the party had given members 40 per cent of the vote for a new leader and affiliated unions 20 per cent. The MPs, with only 40 per cent, could be given a leader most of them did not want, which is what happened. After David Cunliffe was elected, left-wing bloggers believed Cunliffe was their bunny.

Inevitably, the party election attracted public attention and Labour profited in the next polls. The *Herald*-DigiPoll sample in September had National down five points to 43.7 per cent and Labour up nearly seven points to 37 per cent. Add the Greens and Labour would have a majority. John Key's personal rating fell to the lowest point of his premiership, a 'mere' 55.8 per cent. He had been in the 60s and sometimes 70s in DigiPoll surveys, never the 50s.

But Labour's three leadership candidates had made public their fear of Key's political standing. Shane Jones called him 'the $50 million gorilla'. Each of them argued the party needed the best candidate available (him) to have a chance of beating John Key. All of them also stressed that beating National meant getting in the 40 per cents at the election. That would mean Labour was first past the post. By implication, a coalition of second and third past the post, permissible under MMP, would not be a credible government.

After Labour's contest, Key quickly regained his numbers as preferred Prime Minister. In DigiPoll's December survey, he had 61.9 per cent. He is an avid analyst of polls, especially those every government commissions for itself. The Prime Minister's Office polls every week, using a sample of 350 each time. By polling on the same issue over three weeks it can build a sample of 1000 and see changes in the mood week by week. Sometimes it runs a larger poll, with a sample of 1500 people, on a particular issue or a section of the population – Auckland, for example, or women.

Polls in Auckland possibly prompted Key to give much more attention to housing in 2013. House prices, which had fallen only 5 per cent after the bubble burst in 2007, were on a rapid rise again. Key needed to do something for young people trying to buy their first home. Labour was attracting support with a promise to build 100,000 additional state houses over 10 years. Since the abolition of depreciation tax allowances in the 2010 budget had not discouraged property investment, and National would do nothing else to tax demand, it decided to concentrate on the supply side of the house market. It attributed high prices entirely to restrictive land zoning, particularly on the metropolitan periphery where planners were trying to contain urban sprawl.

With Heatley's departure the housing portfolio was handed to Nick Smith, rehabilitated after the Pullar letter disclosure the previous year. Smith might not always have good judgement but he is energetic and can make it appear that something is being done. He was soon meeting Auckland's mayor Len Brown, certain to be re-elected that year, and together they announced an 'accord'. In certain areas of Auckland, designated by the council for development, consents would be processed in three months or six months rather than the usual three years. The council was not given much choice. Smith said the government would take control of the planning and consenting process if they did not achieve the required speed.

Meanwhile, the Reserve Bank was proposing to take action on the demand side, restricting the number of mortgages that banks could issue for more than 80 per cent of the purchase price. Key wanted first-home buyers exempt from the loan-to-value restriction and said so publicly. He also raised the issue with the bank governor, Graeme Wheeler, directly. It was a testing moment for a newly appointed governor. Wheeler had already declared himself against a first-home exemption.

It was also a test of Key's adherence to the bank's statutory independence, one of the foundations of New Zealand's economic stability. Key, it turns out, takes that principle with a grain of salt. 'I knew the politics of it. He's independent but nobody would believe it. They would beat me up on it.' Wheeler held firm in public and with the Prime Minister in private. He was supported by Bill English who, Key has also said publicly, talked him around. However, it is a little disturbing that Key did not, even then, acknowledge the bank's independence.

It is difficult to see why first-home buyers could not at least have been given priority for the 10 per cent of each bank's loans book that were permitted to be above 80 per cent of the property's value. The regulation, primarily designed to reduce retail banking's exposure to higher-risk mortgages, was new territory for the Reserve Bank. Monetary authorities around the world are extending their banking supervision in the wake of the global financial crisis and they are still feeling their way. They can do without public pressure from a Prime Minister.

In March 2014 the Reserve Bank began to raise its base interest rate for the first time since the recession. The economy had taken off on high dairy export prices and the Christchurch rebuild. New Zealand had experienced growth of 3.5 per cent in the previous year and the expansion was forecast to continue through 2014. John Key had a good story to tell when he made his statement to Parliament in January:

> On average, wages are growing faster than inflation. Business confidence is at its highest level since 1999 and the terms of trade are expected to remain high. There are 53,000 more people employed now than a year ago and the unemployment rate is expected to drop further as the economy continues to gather strength.

CHAPTER EIGHTEEN

A Time to Assess

In his sixth year of office John Key's enthusiasm looks and sounds undiminished. Despite 17-hour days, constant movement, numerous speaking engagements, the need to stay in touch with news that moves at frantic pace on digital media, the big black briefcase of papers sent to him every day to be read at any spare moment – at home, in a car, on a plane, at his desk late at night – he is still visibly enjoying the importance and adrenalin of it all. 'The days go incredibly quickly. You never get bored with it.'

Politics has much in common with currency trading. For 15 years he spent his days watching digits move in four decimal places on a screen. The tension and instant decisions traders have to make with vast sums of money at stake keep their eyes fixed on those numbers from dawn to dusk. Lunch is brought to them at their desks; time flies. Key, by all accounts, understood what was driving those numbers at any given time exceptionally well. He learned to trust his instincts completely. He still does.

The numbers he watches now are polls – mainly those he and his staff commission constantly, as all governments do. The decisions Key makes these days are based on a sure instinct for the issues that will move those numbers and the issues that will not. He loses no sleep over most of the topics that make news or generate noise in Parliament, even in some instances filling his message log. Smacking, spying, asset sales are hotly debated but they do not move votes. Others, such as school class sizes, for example, do. Key has no doubt the budget decision was right – the quality of the teacher matters more to a child's education than the number in the class. There is room to increase today's average class size and use the money saved to improve teaching standards. But he says he warned the cabinet they would regret it. When school principals expressed their alarm to parents and an uproar ensued, the currency trader 'exited that position' quickly.

It is unusual for a proposal such as larger classes to see the light of day. Like all prime ministers, Key takes it upon himself to be chief mine detector. When ministers put up a proposal from their department for a cabinet decision, he reads the supporting papers with an eye for any detail that could blow up in his face. Often it is a detail of the method necessary for carrying out the policy which he knows people will find offensive or intrusive. There was just such an explosive buried in a 2014 budget proposal that he would not name. He was astonished that neither the department's officials nor his policy advisory group thought it worth mentioning in their summaries for him. He discovered it in the body of the material and came out of his office saying, 'You guys are barking mad if you think I'm going to sign up to this.'

Key's popularity cannot be measured entirely in votes.

New Zealanders who identify with either National or Labour do not readily switch between them. Political identity is part of a person's self-image, social background, family influence, educational and occupational experiences. When people are content with a government of the 'other' side, they are liable to lend their vote at that election to a smaller party or simply not go to the polls. The comparatively low 77 per cent turnout at the 2002 election was a measure of contentment with Helen Clark, and the 74 per cent turnout in 2011 was probably a sign that many of those who normally vote Labour rather liked John Key.

He is hard not to like. Highly regarded Labour MP Andrew Little got to know him when Little attended Air New Zealand functions as secretary of the Engineering, Printing and Manufacturing Union. Key would turn up as a friend of the airline's then chief executive Rob Fyfe. 'He was pretty affable,' Little found. 'He has got that personable quality which is very effective, no question about that. Around here [Parliament] you can have a good discussion with him out of the public glare.' Little also admires Key's command of the government and his ability to delegate – a contrast, he thinks, to Helen Clark.

> Helen's problem was that being across everything meant controlling everything, whereas, while he is across a lot he clearly has people he can rely on to get stuff done. I think that comes from business. At a senior level in business you get that, you don't get to the level he did without being a good delegator.

But his business credentials are a double-sided coin. They lend credence to the opposition's main point of attack: that Key can be too close to business for the public good, and that policies such as tax cuts, asset sales, the convention centre deal with SkyCity, are for the benefit of 'John Key's mates'. Many of the 'mates Key lates from his business career have been appointed to public bodies, but all governments constantly have positions to fill and draw on those they know. The concern of opponents such as Andrew Little is the process, not the people.

> When you are head of a business you can say, 'I know this person and he will do a good job', but in the public sector there is need for confidence in the process so that it doesn't look like a series of jack-ups. The dinner with SkyCity was too close to the tender process. Likewise the way Ian Fletcher was appointed to head the GCSB. The relationship can look too close. This is a criticism that can be made of Labour too. Ministers should get out of these appointments completely.

There will come a day when a critical mass of voters simply wearies of Key and wants a new face in charge. When he walked off the plane into Wellington Airport on the Monday morning after the 2008 election, people in the terminal clapped as he passed. When he walked through the airport after the election of 2011, it was just another Monday morning. 'It gets harder,' he agrees. 'Things aren't new any more. Time for a change is a massive determining factor in politics and I could be reading this wrong, but I don't think there is any mood for change at the moment.' Helen Clark attended the swearing-in after the 2011 election. 'I don't remember her exact words but she said, "The first term is great; the second is harder; the third is diabolical."' Key feels he is getting better. 'I know I do the job better now than I did in 2008. I know what to look for. I'm much quicker to spot where the bones are going to be buried. What is going to explode. How things are going to work.'

John Key is no longer the fresh-faced financial achiever who came into Parliament talking about making a 'step change' in the New Zealand economy. That phrase disappeared in the fallout from the global financial crisis before he even took office. He never knew precisely what he meant, except that he believed the economy was like an underperforming business that could be generating a higher level of income for all New Zealanders if only its government was prepared to be more daring, such as taking on more debt. He admits he now knows better.

> If you'd asked me when I first went into politics how important was public policy to a country's success on a scale of one to ten – one being not important – I would have said seven. If you ask me now, I'd say 9.5. Because when you look around the world, there are lots of countries with everything going for them and they do really badly, and there are countries that don't have those environments that do incredibly well.

Good public policy, as prescribed by international institutions such as the OECD, is dull. It means controlling government spending and taxation, balancing the budget and maintaining sound monetary conditions for low inflation. Most importantly, it means low government debt. That is the first figure credit agencies want to know when they assess how well a country is governed. The government debt reflects whether the budget has been balanced over a reasonable period. It is not the total national debt which includes private-sector borrowing, and less of a worry in open economies with floating exchange rates. The government's debt is what really matters.

On that score Key's performance is mixed. He inherited a budget heading deep into deficit. Despite the cost of a recession and two destructive earthquakes, he and Bill English expect to post a surplus in 2015, enabling them to project credible debt reductions in the years ahead. They have managed to contain public spending without drastic cuts in any services or the painful economic adjustments of the past.

But Key also inherited a very low public debt from the Labour Government that had enjoyed eight years of economic growth. Labour's legacy was the main reason that National has been able to run up $60 billion of debt since 2008 without putting New Zealand's credit rating and living standards at much risk. With strong growth returning in 2013 to 2014, generating Budget surpluses from 2015, New Zealand has an opportunity to get its public debt down again before the next economic 'shock' occurs. Key seems in no hurry. His Government aims to get the debt back down below 20 per cent of GDP no sooner than 2020. On the eve of its first budgeted surplus, Key said surpluses gave the Government an option to promise tax cuts at the 2014 election weighted to the lower paid. If Key remains in office to 2017 or even 2020, it is doubtful he will leave a public debt as low as the one that Labour left him.

Since 2013 the economy has been booming on the Christchurch rebuild. By March 2014 the country recorded 3 per cent growth, more than the world's leading economies that were still on post-recession monetary stimulants or trying to wean themselves off them. Business confidence in New Zealand was at its highest for 20 years. Average wages had risen 2.8 per cent over the year. Inflation was just 1.6 per cent, though as a precaution the Reserve Bank began raising interest rates in March, the first western central bank to do so since the recession.

The 'rock star' economy was set for even faster expansion in 2014–15 from strong dairy export prices and the $40 billion injection of insurance and government funds into Christchurch. New Zealand could have the fastest-growing economy in the OECD this year, but commodity prices are fickle and the earthquake rebuild is a temporary stimulus. Something more needs to happen if New Zealand's low average income is to rise from near the bottom of the OECD table and start to match those in countries that attract educated young people. Key believes the secret to sustained growth lies in what he calls 'connectedness' to the world.

> New Zealand needs to remain open, efficient and welcoming to foreign capital, students, tourists, people coming to live here. Engaging in that trading world is what is going to make us wealthy. New Zealand is going to be better. I think it's already better. It's a more interesting place being multicultural. People are worrying about their kids staying here and having jobs here. Well, the only way you do that is with international connectedness. We are not going to get wealthy selling things to 4.5 million New Zealanders.

Immigration and its investment are easy targets for populists. Winston Peters had a policy to prevent foreigners buying houses in New Zealand. 'How do you define a foreigner for that purpose?' Key asks.

> At Omaha a Chinese billionaire has bought a place as a weekender for his son who is studying at Auckland University. Rumour has it the boy has been there

once in two years, but he is studying here. Do we bar
him? We are almost certainly going to buy Stephie
an apartment in Paris. We are sick of renting and
she'll be there another three years. Is that a legitimate
purchase? How many people wake up one morning in
Guangzhou and decide to buy a house in Pakuranga?
The best estimates we can get suggest that if you apply
the restrictions they are talking about, it might affect 2
per cent of property purchases.

Among his remaining aims in office are free-trade
agreements with Korea and Europe, and the big prize,
the comprehensive trade and investment charter called
the Trans-Pacific Partnership (TPP). With 11 countries
now in those negotiations, including two of the world's
giant economies, the United States and Japan, a successful
conclusion of the TPP would probably set a higher standard
of trade, investment and intellectual property rights for
the world. New Zealand under Helen Clark was one of
the initiators of the TPP and Key has pushed it further,
particularly with Barack Obama. TPP is so ambitious that
it remains a long shot and the US Congress could unpick
any deal the President makes. But Key gives it a 50–50
chance. 'Obama wants to do it.'

———————

Key is not a 'change agent'. He is a normal, conservative
politician who does not take too many steps ahead of public
opinion. There are times when countries, and companies
and schools, all organisations, need change agents – people
prepared to shake them up with necessary decisions that
have been too hard for the organisation's usual culture.

But these people tend to be permanent revolutionaries by nature – ever restive, even obsessive, for perfection. Sir Roger Douglas was one, Don Brash another. Key refused Brash a place on National's front bench after he replaced him as leader in 2006. He would not have Douglas in his government when Douglas returned to Parliament for ACT in 2008. Good change agents in companies and schools recognise they are not the best people to lead the organisation when it returns to normal.

New Zealand politics was restored to normal by Helen Clark at the turn of the century. She denied the value of much of what the change agents had done, which is a common reaction in organisations that have been under stress, but she did not undo what they had done for the productive economy. Her counter-revolution was limited to the public sector where her government took nascent competitive market forces out of public hospitals, state schools and accident insurance.

Key is maintaining politics as normal, without the reactionary rhetoric of the Clark years. Normality does not mean no progress. Just as the Clark government broadened personal retirement savings with the KiwiSaver scheme and started a public superannuation fund from its budget surpluses, Key's has lowered the taxation of personal and company earnings and drawn more of its revenue from consumption with an increase in GST. It has reduced employers' risk a little with legislation allowing them to hire on 90-day trials. It has partially privatised three power companies so that all four of the economy's big electricity providers are now accountable to the share market. And it is wiring the country with fibre-optic cable to households that do not yet need it. Even critics of the price being charged for existing connections in order to make fibre appealing seem confident the new network will pay off.

Key is also encouraging deep-sea oil and gas exploration in the basins of New Zealand's vast continental shelf. The country above water is just a narrow sliver of a lump of ancient continent that probably contains carbon deposits under the Southern Ocean. But he expects farmland will continue to be the main source of national wealth.

> My view is that the economy is going to develop in areas of competitive advantage. That is food production and anything in land. The big trend in food is entertainment [dining out] and health. That will always be what we do. Tourism will always be part of what we do. I think the services base is changing. When I address a business lunch today there are three or four tables of software developers. We have done a few things that surprised people, like the film incentive. You have to do those things to build parts of your economy, particularly for creative people.

Yet if you ask Key what he considers his most worthwhile legacy may be, he is liable to say social welfare reform. When Ruth Key was bringing up two children in a state house in the 1970s, New Zealand's welfare state did not demand that widows and other sole parents find a job if they could. It was Ruth's choice to work and earn more than a benefit, especially with a debt to repay. John Key often invokes her work ethic and it probably inspires his welfare reforms. His government has made all beneficiaries look for at least part-time work unless they are incapacitated or a sole parent of a child under five. Sole parents must look for full-time work once their youngest child is 14. Ruth, who had low-paid jobs from the time John was seven, would today lose her benefit if she worked 30 or more hours a week but she would probably qualify for the Clark government's Working for Families tax credit until John was 19. Key has made job-seeking the first task of social welfare.

> We have completely redefined the front end of Work and Income. The default position used to be: How do you sign up for a benefit? The default now is: How can you get a job? Or: How can we get you a job before you sign up for a benefit? It's very different.

The welfare system offers job-seekers help with childcare, training, even guidance for their CVs and grooming for job interviews. But it will also now suspend benefits if children aged three or over are not in a pre-school centre or school, enrolled with a GP and up to date with health checks. The enforcer of this 'tough love', Minister for Social Development Paula Bennett, says in the three years the rules have been in force, no parent has had the benefit cut for more than eight weeks.

Key's greatest social reform, though, may be in state housing. If his mother was applying for a state house today she could no longer count on living in it for as long as she wished. The Key government has put an end to lifetime tenancies. State tenants now face a three-yearly review of their income and assets and their ability to pay a market rent. That is uncharacteristically risky politics. Sooner or later an elderly tenant is going to be forced out of the state house that she has regarded as her home for 30 or 40 years, in a community she knows. The fact that a refugee family can make more use of the three-bedroom house she has occupied alone will not reduce the public sympathy for her when she appears on television. That is another of the bombshells Key will have spotted and done his best to defuse. The eviction procedure is slow; a minister can intervene.

Key has rejected the path of deep cuts in the size of government, which costs $70 billion a year, a third of the total economy, drawing not just taxation out of the private sector but employing a high proportion of the educated population as well as physical and financial capital. Nevertheless, he thinks his government has made more economic change than people realise. Former Australian Prime Minister John Howard advised him not to touch GST four weeks before he raised the rate. It is odd how a 'third rail', or untouchable issue, in one country is harmless in the other. Australia is not afraid to tax capital gains on housing.

Without an effective capital gains tax on investment in rental residential property, New Zealand houses will probably continue to be among the most unaffordable in the world as a proportion of average incomes. A capital gains tax is a third rail Key will not touch, yet the subject is not quite as untouchable as it used to be. David Cunliffe put Labour's hand to the rail as its finance spokesman in 2011 and has held it there as leader in 2014. It is a pity Key is not braver. Bill English sounds slightly more amenable to a tax solution to the excessive national investment in residential real estate.

The other glaring gap in John Key's plans is, of course, an answer to the baby boom's superannuation and healthcare costs. Unless he asks the voters to release him from a promise – which they probably would by re-electing him if he asked – he will make no adjustments to the age of entitlement or other terms. At least one National veteran of the reform era, Michelle Boag, hopes ACT will force Key's hand by making changes to national super a bottom-line condition of its support for another term.

Richard Prebble, one of Douglas's fellow change agents in 1984–88, has famously said John Key is the best Prime Minister he has seen. 'I think he is. He is certainly the best on TV. Muldoon smashed people, Lange was very funny. John Key is just absolutely reasonable.' Prebble has a theory that most people who go into politics should not be there.

> Going into politics requires a somewhat egotistical personality, which means you are actually unsuited to it. There are quite a few people in politics who are absolutely unsuitable – it is the last thing they should be doing. But Key is extraordinarily well anchored, very balanced. When he has to answer a leading question and I am sitting there thinking, 'How would I answer that? There is no right answer', he doesn't look stressed or sound stressed and what he says leaves you thinking, 'Well, gee, that's a very sensible answer.'

Prebble, a director of Mainfreight these days, says Key is exceptionally good on trade missions. Mainfreight general manager Don Braid will readily go on a mission if the Prime Minister is leading it.

> Key grasps what each industry is about, the key issues they face in that country, and ensures each person on the mission meets the people they need to meet. He works harder than anyone on the mission and he still has his own job to do. He doesn't stop being Prime Minister because he is away.

But Prebble has one concern.

His strength is also his weakness. You can see John Key is a great trader – he looks at the world as a trader. My worry about him is that he sees everything as a trade. I would like to think I could tell you his set of principles – his moral framework, if I can use that phrase – that he wouldn't trade. I'm not sure he wouldn't look at everything as a trade. That might be a bit harsh.

It is a bit harsh. Key's credibility among businesspeople in New Zealand may prove to be a greater driver of sustained economic improvement than any grand plan or policy initiative or reform programme anybody can conceive. Key thinks 'we have changed the culture a bit in New Zealand to be more confident'.

New Zealanders see we are doing better. They see us on the world stage and people are willing to engage with us. They see these long dole queues in Greece and Spain, and America isn't that flash, even Australia isn't looking as lucky. There's more confidence here now, I reckon.

Bill English calls it 'a structural lift in confidence' and credits a lot of it to Key.

People feel like they have got through a difficult time surprisingly well. They are starting to believe they are quite good at it. How else can you account for an export sector running on an 80 US cents-plus dollar without a large-scale controversy about the exchange rate mechanism? It is because they have become more self-reliant, more confident. I think this is a pay-off for his leadership.

Business is very happy that Key is in the chair – not because they expect favours or even that he is a dealer by nature. Deals such as those with SkyCity, Chorus, the telco line operator doing the ultra-fast broadband roll-out, and Warner Bros. Pictures to make *The Hobbit* here, hardly amount to a wholesale reversion to crony capitalism, corporate welfare, 'picking winners'. John Key inspires confidence because he has been a winner.

All too few corporate leaders come into politics. Even the National Party is often short of people with strong business credentials. Business leaders see politics in all its public rows and heated rhetoric and they wonder, 'Why bother?' Key *has* bothered, and he was no ordinary business leader. He was head of global foreign exchange for one of the big five Wall Street banks and was going to go even higher, when he bothered.

His decision to come back and fulfil an ambition harboured since his youth says much for New Zealand as well as him. It says the country's politics and economic possibilities can excite someone who could take his ambitions anywhere, and it says something about how much he cares for the country he runs. He is not a reformer, not a visionary. He takes as read the important principles of an open, competitive market economy and applies them, but not inflexibly. He knows principles are made to be stretched at times – like a trader going 'long' on a currency – but that like a currency position they must not be stretched too far or too often. New Zealand feels content, stable and successful with a Prime Minister who is easy to like and inspires confidence. If he can carry on like this, the country could be permanently better off and he could yet rank with our best.

Acknowledgements

This book was not John Key's idea, nor mine. The credit belongs to the publisher, Penguin Books, who sensed there was a story to tell about this Prime Minister and the time was ripe to tell it. When the idea was put to me, I readily agreed. Too many political stories go untold until too late.

It is an honour to be trusted with another person's life story. I am grateful to John Key for three long and candid interviews this year, and to Bronagh for joining us for the second of them. I deeply appreciate the willingness of his sisters, Liz Cave and Sue Lazar, to share their memories, some of the earliest being painful. His Chief of Staff, Wayne Eagleson, was an invaluable guide to the inner workings of the government. Deputy Chief of Staff Paula Oliver, previously a colleague on the *New Zealand Herald*, was a vital point of contact throughout. She and another former colleague, Kevin Taylor, provided previously unpublished photographs taken by the Prime Minister's staff.

I wish to thank all of those I have quoted for the thought they gave the subject, and to thank others who were not quoted extensively, if at all, but provided useful background and contacts. Among them are Don Whelan and Paul O'Connor of Burnside High School, and John Hunt, formerly of Bankers Trust, Auckland, who gave me a primer on currency trading. I drew valuable research pointers from the *New Zealand Herald*'s 2008 profile of

John Key by Eugene Bingham, the aforementioned Paula Oliver and Carroll du Chateau.

If this book had footnotes just about every page would be laden with references to the work of *New Zealand Herald* reporters. Access to the archives of a reliable newspaper has been vital to checking my recall of events and their sequence. I have particularly appreciated the interest and at times criticism of the *Herald*'s Editor in Chief, Tim Murphy, the encouragement of its Political Editor Audrey Young and the use of *Herald* photographs compiled with the help of its editorial resources manager Lauri Tapsell.

Above all, I am grateful to Penguin, particularly its General Manager, Publishing, Debra Millar, who proposed the book to me, bolstered my resolve to do it and provided essential production advice along the way. A book in the writing so dominates the mind that it intrudes on the life of a partner too. Cathy's support has been constant, thoughtful and enthusiastic. I appreciate it beyond words.

Index

Abbott, Tony 9
ACC (Accident Compensation
    Corporation) 99, 170, 210
ACT Party 109, 138, 148, 149, 151,
    152, 164–6, 167, 171, 174,
    209, 240
'A Day in the Life of a Foreign
    Exchange Dealer' 63
Air New Zealand 202, 203
All Blacks 155
Alliance 165
America's Cup, Fremantle 68
Anderton, Jim 108–9
Aorangi School 30
APEC meetings 151, 152, 154
Armstrong, John 181–2, 211
Arney Crescent, Remuera 75
asset sales programme 201–206, 212
Auckland Council 171, 226–7
Auckland 'super city' 171
Audit Office 207–8
August Place, Auckland 19
Auxiliary Territorial Service 39

Balmoral Castle 11–13
Bankers Trust 69–74, 75–7
banking crisis, US 143–5
Banks, John 209–11: donation fiasco
    210–11; 'teapot' tape 209–10
Bathurst, Riley 105, 141–2
Bathurst, Tim 105, 141
Bear Stearns 144
Beatson, David 31
Beckham, David 178–9
Beehive 155–9
Bell, Warren 59
Bellotti, Steve 78, 86

Bennett, Paula 138, 181, 239
Bernanke, Ben 144
Big Gay Out festival 178
Bingham, Eugene 70, 155
Binns, Mark 195, 196–7
Birch, Bill 63, 92, 160
Blair, Tony 100, 130
Blue, Jackie 135, 136
Boag, Michelle 93–4, 95–6, 98, 102–3,
    107, 147, 240
Bolger, Jim 150, 151, 153
Bono 15
Borkin, Philip 197
Bowler, Kevin 179
Bradford, Max 108
Bradford, Sue 138, 172
Braid, Don 241
Brash, Don 73, 94, 106, 109, 113–14,
    129–31, 132, 151, 163, 165–6,
    178, 237: Orewa speech 113–14
Breakfast programme 157, 219
Bridges, Simon 148, 216
Brierley Investments 68
Brown, Gordon 130, 155
Brown, Len 226–7
Brownlee, Gerry 107, 109, 131, 157,
    192, 200
Burgess, Malcolm 209
Burnside High School 27, 49–52
Burnside rugby club 34, 133
Bush, George W. 154
business confidence 228, 234–5
Business Roundtable 118
businesspeople and politics 242–3

cabinet committees 166–7
cabinet meetings 155–7

Cameron, David 11
Campbell Live programme 136
Canterbury Earthquake Recovery
    Authority (CERA) 195
Canterbury Employers' Chamber of
    Commerce 192
Canterbury International 60–1
Canterbury University 51, 55
Capital Markets Bank, Ireland 87
Catherine, Duchess of Cambridge
    (Kate) 11, 12, 13
caucus meetings 108, 131, 175
Cave, Liz (née Key) 18, 20, 21, 22–5,
    28, 29, 30, 32, 39, 41–2, 43, 44,
    46, 60, 92, 105–6
Cave, Milly 105, 141
Cave, Roger 46, 105, 141
Caygill, David 71
Chancery Lane, Singapore 77
charter schools proposal 174
Chorus 243
Christchurch earthquakes 23, 189–93,
    195–7: assistance to businesses
    192; economic effects 196–7, 234
Christchurch synagogue 41–2
Christchurch Town Hall 144
Citibank 79
Clarendon Hotel 22, 23, 28, 30
Clark, Helen 58, 93, 99–101, 114,
    115, 129, 135, 138, 142–3,
    144–5, 149, 150, 152–3, 158,
    166–7, 168, 174–5, 202, 203,
    231, 232, 237: competency 93;
    delegating 231
Clarkson, Bob 148
Clements, Robin 53, 58–9
Close Up programme 67–8, 135–6
coalitions, parliamentary 165, 174
Cobham Intermediate School 33, 34
Collins, Judith 94, 106, 222, 225
Collins, Paul 68
confidence and supply
    arrangements 168
Connell, Brian 106
Contact Energy 203
Cornwall Park District School 20

Costello, Peter 130
Crafer farms sale 210
Creech, Wyatt 108
Cullen, Michael 99–100, 132, 140,
    144–5, 183, 184
Cumming, Geoff 145–6
Cunliffe, David 97, 194, 225, 240

Davison, Paul 211
Deloittes 59
Development Finance Corporation
    64–5
Devine, Cecil 52
Dingle Dell, St Heliers 17
dollar, NZ 62, 63–4, 68, 71–2, 242:
    floating 63–4
Dominion Post 223
Donnelly, Gary 25
Dotcom, Kim 210–12, 222, 223–4
Douglas, Roger 61–2, 63, 71, 72, 166,
    202, 237
Duff, Robin 50–1
Dunne, Peter 100–101, 147, 151,
    152, 160–1, 164, 166–8, 170,
    174–5, 222–3

Eagleson, Wayne 10, 151, 152–3, 156,
    159, 167, 216, 223
Earnslaw Crescent 28
Earthquake Commission (EQC) 192
earthquakes *see* Christchurch
economic change 24–5, 236–8,
    239–40: growth 234–5
Edwards, Brian 31, 142
Elders Merchant Finance 65, 66–9
elections (2002) 93, 98, 100; (2008)
    141–50; (2011) 205–6; (2014)
    103, 163, 216–17; post-election
    negotiations 163–75
Electoral Act 101, 165
Electricity Corporation 203
electricity market 203–5, 237
Elizabeth House, Merivale 62
employment legislation 237
English, Bill 93, 109, 113, 131, 145,
    157, 162, 166, 174, 183–4, 197–

9, 200, 203, 206, 221, 227, 240, 242: as finance minister 197–9; and polls 206
Equiticorp 70
exchange rates 99, 118, 122, 233, 242

Farish, Judge Jane 194
Federal Reserve (US) 144
Fendalton, Christchurch 34
Field, Taito Phillip 129, 138
Fischer, Heinz 39–40
Flavell, Te Ururoa 174
Fleming, Stephen 180
Fletcher Building 195
Fletcher, Ian 232
Foreman, Nicky 156
forex (foreign exchange/currency) dealers 64–9
Fresh FM, Nelson 131
Fyfe, Rob 231

gambling 207–8
García, Alan 154
Gardiner, Wira 114
Genesis Energy 203, 205
George, Garth 182
Glade Avenue, Christchurch 22–3
global financial crisis (GFC) 153, 183–5, 203, 227, 233
Goff, Phil 158, 205
Going, Sid 34
Goldman Sachs 79–80, 197
Goudie, Sandra 106
Government Communications Security Bureau (GCSB) 211, 213, 223–4, 232
Green Party 100–101, 169, 204, 225
Green, Garry 95–6
Groser, Tim 152
Guy, Nathan 224

Hager, Nicky: *The Hollow Men* 130
Hague, Kevin 178
Hanmer Springs 105
Harawira, Hone 172
Harbour Lights restaurant 20, 25–6

Harvard University 87
Havelock North 22
Hawaii 9–10, 13
Hawkins, Allan 70
healthcare 240
Heatley, Phil 215
Helensville electorate 94–8, 101–103, 109, 148: candidate selection 94–6; living out of electorate 96–7, 101–102
Henare, Tau 171
Herald on Sunday 209, 219
Herlihy, Gavin 108
Hide, Rodney 138, 148, 151, 152, 164, 167, 170, 171
Highsted Road, Christchurch 43
Hill Cone, Deborah 173
Hitler, Adolph 37–8, 41
Hobbit, The (film) 222
Holland, Sidney 121
Hollyford Avenue, Christchurch 27, 28, 42
Holmes programme 178
Holocaust 35, 41
Holyoake, Keith 31, 150, 220
home mortgages 139, 227
Hooker Avenue, Christchurch 28
housing affordability 138–9, 226, 227, 240
Howard, John 130, 140, 240
Hu Jintao 154
Hughes, Rob 53, 54, 56
Hunt, John 85–6

immigration 235
inflation 59, 228, 234
interest rates 228
internet access 237
Ireland, Aroha 135–6
iwi leaders' forum 173–4

Jarrett, Ken 70
Jellie Park 27
Jewish persecution 37–9, 41
Johnson, Boris 155
Johnston, Grant 180

Jones, Paul Tudor 68
Jones, Shane 225
Joyce, Steven 157, 162, 208, 221 2

Karpeles, Charlotte ('Lottie'; later
    Charlotte Weiss) 38–9, 41, 46
Kaye, Nikki 148, 178, 216
Kerr, Roger 118, 152
Key, John: accountancy 56–7, 59–60;
    ambitions 32, 33, 34, 35, 47, 53,
    86; and 'anti-smacking' bill 137–8;
    associate finance spokesman
    113; backbench MP 105–15;
    Bronagh, meeting 54–5; cabinet
    administration 155–7; catwalk
    stunt 181; class sizes 230; and
    conscience votes 111–12; cooking
    39, 220; cricket 180; 'crony
    capitalism' 117–27, 231–2, 242;
    currency dealer 14, 63–74, 75–89,
    229; debating 51–2; early life 14,
    19–26, 49–62; and economics
    53–4, 56–7; education 14, 20, 22,
    33, 34, 49–58; electorate 94–103;
    and father 24–5; foreshore/
    seabed legislation 112–13, 172;
    future 217–18, 220–2; golf
    9–10, 34, 161–2; holiday homes
    10, 88; horse racing 52–3; and
    immigration 235; income 52,
    74, 81–2, 83–4, 88–9; Jewish
    ancestry 41; lifestyle block 101;
    maiden speech 105–6; and Maori
    112, 132–3, 163–74; ministerial
    reshuffles 215–17; oratory 142;
    paper round 34; party leader,
    elected 131–40; personality 13–14,
    15, 35, 58, 86, 161, 182; politics,
    entering 91–103; popularity 13–
    14, 177–87, 201, 205, 221, 230–1;
    post-election negotiations 163–75;
    press conferences 157–8; Prime
    Minister, elected 48–50; privacy/
    security 218–19; and privatisation
    200–203, 222; and prostitution law
    reform 111–12; public speaking
    51, 91, 132, 133–4; publicity stunts
    178–82; rugby 34–5; and same-sex
    marriages 112, 178; school subjects
    49–50, 53; and snapper quota 224–
    5; and social welfare 133, 238–9;
    sports 34–5, 58, 180; squash 58–9,
    133; and state housing 110–11,
    226–7, 239; and 'underclass'
    133, 134–7; university 14, 55–9;
    wedding 62; and Whenuapai air
    base 110–11; working routine
    155–62, 217–18, 229
Key, Bronagh (née Dougan) 11–12,
    15, 54–5, 58, 60, 63, 64, 66, 77–8,
    80–1, 82–3, 89, 97, 101, 141, 149,
    160, 179, 200, 212–13, 218–20
Key, George 18–24
Key, Martyn 155
Key, Max 10, 11–12, 15, 18–26,
    77, 84, 89, 97, 141, 149, 160,
    178, 220
Key, Ruth (née Lazar) 28–35, 37–47,
    57, 58, 106, 111, 238: dinner-
    table debates 30–2, 33, 52; faith
    41–2; funeral 47; smoking 33–4
Key, Stephanie (Stephie) 11–12, 13,
    77, 89, 97, 141, 149, 160, 219–20
Key, Sue see Lazar, Sue
Kidd, Doug 108
King, Ben 10
King's College 160–1
Kirk, David 95
Kirk, Norman 32, 150
Kitteridge, Rebecca 222
Kiwibank 146
KiwiRail 146
KiwiSaver 139, 146, 237
Knowledge Wave 100
Krieger, Andy 71
Kumeu 94; see also Helensville
Kyd, Warren 94, 108

Labor Party (Australia) 121, 140
Labour Party 32, 70, 99, 165, 169, 199,
    201–2, 204, 225, 226, 240
Lane Walker Rudkin 60, 65, 92

Lange, David 62, 64, 71, 142, 150, 201–2
Lazar, Herbert 37, 39, 41
Lazar, Herta 41
Lazar, Irma (née Wodak) 40–1
Lazar, Jacques 37, 38, 40
Lazar, Leo 40–1
Lazar, Margarethe (Greta) 37, 38–9, 41
Lazar, Mathilde 40
Lazar, Max 37
Lazar, Norbert 37, 38, 40
Lazar, Sue (née Key) 17, 19, 20, 21, 24, 28, 30–4, 39, 42–3, 44, 45–7, 52, 105–6, 141, 150, 219
Lee Hsien Loong 154
Lehman Brothers 144, 183–4
Letterman, David: *Late Show with David Letterman* 179–80
Liberal Party (Australia) 121
Little, Andrew 231, 232
London, living in 78–82
Lotu-Iiga, Sam 217
Luxton, John 108

'M1' money supply figure 85
Maharey, Steve 135
Mahuika, Api 173
Mallard, Trevor 129–30
Mana Party 172
Mandela, Nelson, funeral 9–10, 15
Maori 112–15, 132–3, 163–74: and Don Brash 113–15; foreshore and seabed legislation 112–15, 172; iwi leaders' forum 173–4; Treaty of Waitangi 114, 115, 164, 210
Maori Party 115, 151, 152, 163–74, 210
Martin, G. Kelly 86, 88
McCann, Ewen 56
McCarten, Matt 172
McClay, Todd 148
McCulloch Menzies 59
McCully, Murray 39, 131, 152, 157
McGehan Close, Auckland 134–7
McLay, Jim 62, 108–9

Megaupload 210
Meridian Energy 203, 205
Merrill Lynch 77, 78–82, 84–8, 144, 216
Merrill Lynch Wealth Management 87–8
Mighty River Power 203, 204–5
mining 186, 187
Ministry of Business, Innovation and Employment 194
Minto, John 172
MMP 100, 164, 221, 225
monetarism 56
Monk, Bernie 195
Moody's Investors Service 197
Morgan Stanley 79, 80
Morgan, Tuku 173
Muck, Ernst 38, 40
Muldoon, Robert 31, 32, 35, 54, 59–62, 150: snap election 61–2; wage-price freeze 59–60

Nathan, Joan 134, 135, 136
National Business Review (NBR) 'Rich List' 81–2
National Party 31, 91–3, 99, 109, 129–30, 149, 165
National Security Agency (US) 223
Nazi Party 37–38, 40, 41
Neeson, Brian 94, 95, 96–8
Newstalk ZB 157
New York, living in 75
New Zealand First 149, 165, 169
New Zealand Herald 70, 136, 145–6, 154, 155, 178, 182
New Zealand Maori Council 212
New Zealand Oil & Gas 194
Nicholson, Marvin 10
Norton, Lois 44–5
Norton, Roger 34, 35, 44–5, 46–7, 58, 108
Novopay problems 212, 222
nuclear-free New Zealand 146
Nugent Royale (horse) 53

O'Sullivan, Fran 119

Obama, Barack 9–11, 12, 142, 149, 236
oil and gas exploration 238
Omaha beach house 88
Opua, Bay of Islands 18–19
Oriana (ship) 30
Orsman, Bernard 96–7
Overseas Investment Office 210

Packer, Michael 88
Palmer, Geoffrey 178
Parata, Hekia 114, 173
Parker, Bob 191
Parkin, Rae 135
Parnell, living in 83–4, 88–9, 97, 101, 141–2, 218–19
Peters, Winston 147–8, 152, 175, 235
Phillipson, Dave 60, 61
Pike River Coal 194
Pike River Mine disaster 190, 193–5
pokies (poker machines) 207–8
polls 93, 113, 114, 137, 139–40, 142, 181–2, 186, 204, 206, 208, 211–12, 225, 226, 230
post-election negotiations 163–75
Power, Simon 110, 131, 217
Prebble, Richard 107, 240–1
Premier House 160, 161, 162, 218
press conferences 157–8
Prince Philip, Duke of Edinburgh 12
privatisation 200–3, 222
Problem Gambling Foundation 207
public expenditure 197–9, 233–4, 237
public–private partnerships (PPPs) 120
Pullar, Bronwyn 210
Pulu, Charlie 134

Queen Elizabeth II 11–13

Reserve Bank 139, 227, 228, 234
Resource Management Act amendment 169
Rich, Katherine 112, 137–8
Richards, Paul 70

Richardson, Ruth 121–2
Richmond Primary School 22
Rio Tinto 204
Robertson, Julian 68
Rockefeller, Herman 68
Rockhouse, Daniel 194
Rogernomics 118
Rosenberg, Wolfgang 56
Rowling, Bill 32, 86
Roy, Heather 138, 164
Rudd, Kevin 140, 158
Russley Hotel 54–5
Ryall, Tony 217

Salmond, Anne 223
same-sex adoption 178
same-sex marriage 111, 178, 221
Savage, Michael Joseph 218
school class sizes 230
September 11 attack 88
Sharples, Pita 115, 163–4, 167, 170, 173
Shearer, David 224–5
Shipley, Jenny 91–3, 108, 115–16
Simich, Clem 95, 112
Simmeringer Lederwerke Gebrüder Lazar 37
Simpson, Heather 153
Simpson, Scott 96
Singapore, living in 75–7
six o'clock closing 20–1
SkyCity 145, 149, 206–8, 232: convention centre deal 206–8, 232
Slater, John 92, 93
Smith, Nick 170, 210, 226
Smith, Phillippa 208
Smith, Russell 194
snapper quota 224–5
social welfare reform 133
Solid Energy 203, 222
Solomon, Mark 173
South Canterbury Finance 187
Springbok tour (1981) 30–1, 57, 59
St Aidan's Anglican Church, Christchurch 41

St Heliers, Auckland 17
St Stephens Avenue, Parnell, Auckland 83–4, 88–9, 97, 101, 141–2, 218–19
state tenants 239
student loans 146, 147, 153
superannuation 146, 147, 153–4
synagogue, Christchurch 41–2

Taiaroa, Archie 173
Tau, Sonny 173
tax 166, 183–5, 204, 226, 237, 239, 240: capital gains 204, 240; cuts 166; GST 185–6, 237, 239, 240; working group 185
Tay, Frank 57
'Teagate' tape recording 209–10
Te Heuheu, Georgina 114–15
Te Heuheu, Tumu 173
Te Tii marae 115
terms of trade 228
Thatcher, Margaret 56
Thompson, Jason 134
Tibble, Tiwana 208
Tiwai Point aluminium smelter 204, 222
Tizard, Judith 148
Tonkin & Taylor Ltd 192–3
Tourism New Zealand 179
Townsend, Peter 192
Trans-Pacific Partnership (TPP) 236
Tranz Rail 142
Treasury 62, 159, 183, 185, 197
Treaty of Waitangi 114, 115, 164, 210
Tremain, Chris 216
Turia, Tariana 113, 115, 163–4, 165, 167, 171–3

unemployment rate 54, 117, 123–4, 192, 228
Unite 219
United Future 100, 152, 169
United Nations Declaration of the Rights of Indigenous Peoples 172
Upston, Louise 148

van Dijk, Robert 178
Vance, Andrea 223
Vienna, Austria 37–40, 45

wages 228, 234
Wailea resort, Maui holiday home 88
Waimauku lifestyle block 101
Waitangi Day 115, 135, 172
Waitangi Tribunal 212
Walker, Gavin 69, 71, 72, 76, 77, 85, 86, 88
Wall, Louisa 112
Wall Street 79, 87, 144
Walsley, Chris 58, 59
Warne, Shane 180
Warner Bros. 222
Weekend Herald 96
Wellington, living in 22, 66–9
Wereta, Tumanako 173
Western Leader 101
Wevers, Maarten 153
Whanau Ora 172
Whenuapai air base 110–11
Wilkinson, Kate 194, 215
William, Prince, Duke of Cambridge 11, 12, 13
Williams, Mike 145
Williamson, Maurice 107
Wilson, Margaret 130
Wolf of Wall Street, The (film) 84
Wong, Pansy 112, 148
Work and Income 238–9
Working for Families 139, 146, 147, 183, 206, 239
Worth, Richard 101

Young, Audrey 154, 165

Ziller, George 65–6

About the Author

John Roughan is a journalist who has been observing and writing on New Zealand politics for the past 40 years. Born in Southland and educated in Christchurch, he graduated from Canterbury University with a degree in history and a diploma in journalism. He began his newspaper career on the *Auckland Star* before travelling extensively, working on newspapers in Japan and the United Kingdom at the time of the election of Margaret Thatcher.

On his return to New Zealand, he joined the *New Zealand Herald* and was posted to the parliamentary press gallery in Wellington, where he covered the dramatic final years of the Muldoon era and the beginning of the Lange–Douglas Government's rapid reforms of the New Zealand economy.

In 1988 he became the *Herald*'s chief editorial writer, and in 1996 he was invited to write a weekly column which continues to appear in the *Weekend Herald*. Roughan won the Qantas Media Award for editorial writing in 2000, 2001 and 2003, and was named the Qantas Media Awards' best political columnist in 2000 and best general columnist in 2003. In that year he was also awarded the Qantas Fellowship to Wolfson College, Cambridge; a term of study at the university which he took up in 2005.

Roughan lives in Auckland with his wife Cathy and has two grown-up children and two grandchildren.